THE STRUGGLE FOR EQUALITY

THE STRUGGLE FOR EQUALITY

School Integration Controversy
in New York City

By

BERT E. SWANSON

Professor of Political Sociology and Coordinator
Institute for Community Studies
Sarah Lawrence College

With a FOREWORD by

BERT JAMES LOEWENBERG

Professor of History and Director Center for Continuing
Education and Community Studies, Sarah Lawrence College

HOBBS, DORMAN & COMPANY, INC.
New York   Buenos Aires

FOREWORD

Desegregation of the American school system transcends the issues of public education. The struggle for equality is the struggle of men and women everywhere. Only the historical conditions and the specific participants differ. The history of democracy is the history of dissolving the cultural and psychological limitations inhibiting human development. Discriminatory barriers of caste and class, of intellectual and institutional blockages to equality impede its fulfillment. Equality of opportunity is the precondition of human growth.

Demands for desegregation in the public schools continue to evoke conflict vital to democracy and the modes of its operation. The conflict in the city of New York, first fully discussed in the following pages, has a significance beyond the particular dialectics of local disputants and beyond the confines of the metropolitan area. No American community can elude the thrust of civil rights groups to achieve equality of educational opportunity; no American city can escape the political and social dissension involved in the efforts to achieve it. A decade of struggle in the largest American urban center foreshadows the shape of controversy and the probable lines of solution elsewhere. It outlines the nature of group antagonisms, the contagion of conflict, the unspoken urges of threatened ethnic, social and political elements in diversified societies. Whatever may appear on the surface of debate, the urban context of the school has altered it. Disagreements may be denominated political, but politics and power suggest latent drives as well as overt actions.

Brown vs the Boards of Education, the classic Supreme Court ruling on integration of 1954, finally adjusted the letter of the Constitution of the United States to the spirit of the Preamble of the Declaration of Independence. The Preamble of the Declaration of Independence is the clearest statement of the American faith. American history is the record of attempts to translate its principles into legal and social fact. If the tender-minded often dismiss Thomas Jefferson's injunctions as vain sentimentality, the tough-minded have made them the objectives of purposeful democratic change.

Bronxville, New York
January, 1966.

Bert James Loewenberg

PREFACE

This is a final report of a year spent in exploring the problems and decision-making processes associated with the integration of public schools in the largest city in the United States. The difficulty in studying a very large system was made more complex by a surprising level of community controversy in a northern city believed to be one of the most tolerant in the nation. We witnessed: (1) an attempt to introduce the Princeton Plan pairing of adjoining, predominantly white and predominantly minority group schools; (2) a white boycott in opposition to this program; and (3) the dismissal of a Superintendent with a national reputation.

All these events were part of the struggle for equality now associated with the Negro civil rights movement. But they also flowed from the traditional commitment, both ideological and legal, to the democratic ethos of equality, as well as from another basic American value, achievement. The American public school system is believed to be a major agent in fostering both.

This generation is confronted by the dramatic consequences of the paradoxical quest for equality and achievement. That is, in order to *be* equal, people need the opportunity to *become* equal, regardless of birth, class, or race. However, differential levels of achieved status in our society have come to affect basically the equality of opportunity, and inequalities have crept into our society and schools. School officials in particular become painfully aware of this fault as demands are made upon them to initiate corrective measures. To bring about the necessary change, however, will involve not only educational policy but also political power. In a sense, then, our school superintendents have "inherited a revolution" that they were hardly prepared to lead. Their problem is to make the school an effective instrument to counter the strong preferences for segregated neighborhoods as well as discriminating patterns of work and play with one's own kind.

This study concentrated on the reaction of the dominant white community to proposed integration policies. Their schools were being "invaded," their power was challenged. As our research continues, the fuller picture of demands and counterdemands, as well as the roles of the rulers and the ruled, will be developed.

Establishing a field operation under these circumstances was difficult. Considerable time and energy was used to develop communications with key influentials and participants in the educational arena. This situation required of the research staff a flexible approach and an open mind in order to insure the opportunities to seek information at its source and glean the richness of the materials collected, assembled, and analyzed. Acknowledgment is due David Rogers who helped develop the citywide materials; Lawrence Menard, Rozlyn Menzel, Barry Novak, Joy Dryfoos, Madelyn Peritz, Marjorie Silverman, and Jane Winer, who helped in the search for some meaning of the subcommunity; and Jean Swanson, Lillian Farber, and Susan Scarpelli, who helped in the preparation of this final report. The author wishes to thank the following people for their helpful criticism: Naomi Block, Deborah Hensler, Leon Cohen, Burton Onstine, and Blanche Blank.

Special acknowledgment should be given to the numerous participants in the integration controversy who were kind enough to give their time and share their thoughts, experiences, and insights with us. The interpretations contained in the present report, of course, are those of the writer.

The research reported herein was supported by the Cooperative Research Program of the Office of Education, U.S. Department of Health, Education, and Welfare, as Cooperative Research Project No. 2857.

Bronxville, New York
January, 1966

Bert E. Swanson, Coordinator
Institute for Community Studies
Sarah Lawrence College

CONTENTS

CHAPTER

Chapter 1

SCOPE AND METHOD

INTRODUCTION

Segregation of our schools has become a national problem, as enunciated in the 1954 United States Supreme Court decision. But it is at the local--the community rather than the national--level that school integration plans actually are formulated and that citizens and interest groups react to any particular integration efforts. Here one can witness in bold relief the variety of intergroup conflicts along class, racial, religious, ethnic, and other lines over such matters as the desirability of integration and (where it is accepted as desirable) the appropriate speed, degree, and type. At this level school administrators, school board members, teachers, parents' groups, politicians, and other interested parties engage in a struggle that will involve our society for decades to come, namely, how to shape the character of this major change in our educational institutions. Indeed, if one were to list the issues that most provoke conflict and controversy in American cities--urban renewal, housing, fluoridation, metropolitan reorganization--there would be wide agreement that school integration most concerns the whole community.

The major problem of this preparatory research program has been to ascertain the feasibility of a full-scale study of the dynamics of school integration controversies in New York City. So little systematic research has been done on school integration controversies, especially those in big northern cities, that virtually no developed models existed to suggest hypotheses about the stages through which such a controversy is likely to proceed and the effects of different social and cultural contexts on its possible course. James Coleman, for example, suggests:

> We do not know, on the basis of present evidence, <u>what kinds</u> of ties are strongest in a controversy. An important research question would be this: Where do the lines of cleavage come in a community containing many kinds of cross-cutting social attachments? That is, which relations are most easily broken? Answers to these questions would

1

allow us to make much more accurate predictions
than at present of the course of controversy and
the ultimate lines of cleavage. [1]

The research objectives were twofold. The first was to
construct a political or structural map, identifying significant
leaders in integration controversies, their organizational bases,
and their over-all objectives. This would include a delineation
of (1) the extent and types of change in alliances and rivalries
over time; (2) what events, episodes, or conditions give rise to
whatever stability or change were found, and (3) what consequences ensue from such interest group alignments as they impinge on decisions as to what integration efforts are made, where,
and with what expected results. The second objective was to investigate the availability of various types of data for a full-scale
study. This includes an examination of (1) the numerous data
sources in the community; (2) the reliability of this material; and
(3) the value and relevance of these data to the selection of the
significant variables in explaining the integration processes.

The more general implications of the preliminary study had
both a policy and a basic social science nature. The study was
directly relevant to policy in its concern to understand how school
integration policies are established, at both citywide and state
levels, and why local neighborhood reactions take the form they
do. The existence of so much intergroup conflict suggested either
that educational administrators have some misconceptions of how
the citizenry will respond when such a major social change is
introduced, or that local conditions--e.g., segregated housing--
are such that no plans and techniques for introducing change can
be implemented without considerable resistance and conflict.

Unfortunately for educational administrators, social science
conceptions or models of big city politics (more specifically of
educational politics) offer little or no help in suggesting the conditions for effective school integration plans for northern schools.
By definition the dynamics of integration in the North differ from
desegregation processes in the South where most of the research
has been done. In addition, there is a difference in the degree if
not in the kind of integration of schools in small cities (again we
had some data) than in large ones. It was hoped that a better

---

[1]James S. Coleman, Community Conflict (Glencoe, Ill.: The
Free Press, 1957), p. 18.

2

understanding of these processes might be gained from this study of integration in New York City.

In addition to such obvious social policy implications are those of more academic relevance, especially as they contribute to knowledge in the community power or city politics field. Several issues have been in the forefront of developments in that field. First, there was much discussion of the relative merits of various procedures or techniques for studying power. Recently, more substantive concerns were widely discussed, especially the comparative question of specifying the conditions under which a community has a more monolithic or pluralistic power structure. A further issue, pertaining to the extent of effectiveness of political leadership, is in what kinds of communities, with what political forms and leaders, and on what kinds of issues does one find high or low levels of effectiveness in solving some important citywide problems. This seems to be the major issue of integration in New York City--namely, why have the Board of Education and other political leaders been so ineffectual in integrating the city schools? What circumstances in New York City preclude any orderly solution to the problem?

This is not just a New York City problem. Indeed, it may become one of the biggest problems of our "mass society." One prevalent model of the mass society, espoused by such distinguished thinkers as De Tocqueville, Ortega y Gasset, and Lippmann, is that in an increasingly democratic society the mass pressures on leaders will be so great as to foster a definite decline in leadership. Morris Janowitz recently expressed this:

> Everywhere community leadership faces a common problem, namely, the issue is not manipulation of the citizenry by a small elite, but rather the inability of elites to create the conditions required for making decisions. [1]

While this is the problem of many other American communities, in New York City more knowledge is needed about the conditions which make the problem greater or less. Here efforts are being made to provide an effective answer to the integration of the public school system. New York is willing to search for and

---

[1]Morris Janowitz, Community Political Systems (Glencoe, Ill.: The Free Press, 1961), p. 17.

3

experiment with new proposals and methods of implementing them.

In many ways New York sets the pattern for the nation. New York's successes and failures are taken into consideration by other cities when they reach the stage of setting up plans and implementing them on a selective community basis. Previous work in public housing and urban renewal, for example, has made it quite clear that national policy is fashioned after the needs and articulated demands of this city. Eventually, by developing a theoretical model, the New York experience can lead to the kinds of propositions and generalizations that may be applicable in other large urban centers.

BACKGROUND OF INTEGRATION IN NEW YORK

A brief overview of the recent integration events in New York will illustrate the relation of the research interests expressed here and the educational problems. The integration of New York schools began in earnest when the Skipwith case[1] presented the school administration with a specific and embarrassing situation. In the Domestic Relations Court the Board of Education proceeded to declare Negro parents guilty of neglect because they withdrew their children from school in protest against allegedly inferior schools. The court found the parents not guilty of neglect and upheld their right to refuse to obey the New York compulsory education law. The court believed that the city's racially segregated schools had in fact become inferior.

Prior to this decision and shortly after the 1954 Supreme Court decision, however, school leaders began to formulate a set of specific programs in response to demands to end de facto school segregation and inequality of educational opportunity for Negroes and Puerto Ricans. The School Board was disturbed to learn of

> . . . the steady deterioration during the preceding twenty years of the education available to Negro and Puerto Rican children, the disastrously rapid turnover of teachers in the "difficult" segregated schools of the Negro and Puerto Rican neighborhoods;

---

[1]*In the Matter of Skipwith*, 180 N.Y.S. 2d 852 (Dom. Rel. Ct. N.Y.C. 1958), 4 Race Rel. L. Rep. 264 (1959).

the paucity of classes for the intellectually gifted;
the large number of drop-outs among Negro and
Puerto Rican students; the small number entering
college or participating in the Board of Education's
school-work program. [1]

The Board created a Commission on Integration which recommended: (1) raising educational standards and curriculum in economically depressed areas; (2) providing additional guidance, educational stimulation, and job placement for students; (3) improving the physical plant and maintenance of "x"[2] schools and selection of new school sites which would facilitate mixed ethnic enrollment; (4) scheduling of teacher assignments and other personnel to equalize staffing of the schools; (5) integrating through zoning practices; and (6) expanding a centralized community (human) relations unit to guide citizen participation in the problem. [3]

Gradually the Board has begun to implement these recommendations. Rezoning of attendance boundaries in order to designate the schools in big northern cities is complicated by the highly segregated residential patterns. Nevertheless, New York has been able to transfer some 50,000 pupils from overcrowded to underutilized schools with this program. Since most of the overcrowded schools were minority-populated, inevitably some desegregation occurred. This step was considered insufficient and too gradual, however, and the "Open Enrollment Program" was adopted in a more forthright effort to integrate. Under this plan minority group students are permitted to apply for admission to white schools. To date some 15,000 students, both Negro and

---

[1]Board of Education of the City of New York, Toward the Integration of Our Schools (Final Report of the Commission on Integration), June 13, 1958, pp. 5-6.

[2]An "x" (minority) school comprises a Negro and Puerto Rican population of 90 per cent for the elementary schools and 85 per cent for the junior high schools. The "y" (majority) elementary or junior high schools have a Negro and Puerto Rican population of less than 10 or 15 per cent respectively.

[3]For a progress report on these programs, see Board of Education of the City of New York, Toward Greater Opportunity (A Progress Report from The Superintendent of Schools to the Board of Education dealing with Implementation of Recommendations of the Commission on Integration), June, 1960.

Puerto Rican, have taken the opportunity to transfer out of "x" (minority) to "y" (majority) schools.

In June, 1963, the New York State Commissioner of Education issued an order to desegregate all de facto segregated public school systems in the state. The New York City Board of Education responded with a Plan for Integration estimated to cost some ten million dollars a year. This plan provided a list of activities and programs presently in operation, those already scheduled for some time in the future, and those being considered for possible adoption. The list includes:

1. Open enrollment program
2. Free-choice transfer policy (changes the concept of available space to more than 100 per cent, since minority schools are running at 130 per cent)
3. Rezoning in critical fringe areas (Princeton Plan)
4. High school dezoning
5. "Reverse open enrollment" (sending whites into minority schools
6. Establishment of educational parks (large campus sites designed to serve all levels of education)
7. Establishment of special-purpose integrated schools in de facto segregated areas.
8. Human relations training for teachers and supervisors
9. Parent and community education
10. Extended use of group discussion techniques
11. Recruitment of more Negro and Puerto Rican teachers and supervisors
12. Crash remedial and tutorial programs
13. Teaching about minority group contributions to American history and culture
14. Extension of guidance services
15. Strong enforcement of contract provisions against contractors, firms, and suppliers who discriminate

The civil rights groups, however, pronounced the Plan for Integration insufficient and not swift enough. These groups also believed that the Plan should be more specific and include a precise timetable. The School Board's failure to respond to this criticism resulted in two boycotts and the threat of more to come.

The Board's nonresponsive position in the first boycott and the apparent noninvolvement of the city administration disappointed most civil rights leaders. The second boycott, however, was marked by a serious split in the civil rights groups as well as a series of counterdemands and demonstrations by members of the white community (parents and taxpayers groups in particular). The latter vigorously resisted many elements of the Plan, especially the threat to the neighborhood school concept if white children were sent to Negro schools on a nonvoluntary basis. Unexpected resistance came more recently from the supervisory personnel, who object to a major reorganization of the schools.

Their vigorous pursuit of the Plan for Integration makes the school administrator and his staff potential and major innovators in urban life. Together with urban renewal, public health, and social welfare administrators, school administrators are among the most significant public agents for social change in New York. Furthermore, they are dealing with perhaps the most complex, sensitive, and deeply felt social problem in American history. They operate in a vast bureaucratic structure wherein they attempt to gain acceptance by the teachers and administrative personnel further down in the hierarchy who may or may not agree with integration. At the same time the administrators are subject to the will of various lay leaders on school boards and in educational associations, political leaders in the city administration and political parties, and local community leaders who often are uninformed about or unsympathetic to the objectives of integration.

Against this background of Negro demands for desegregation and white citizen resistance, the school leaders have found themselves in the increasingly difficult position of balancing the forces favoring change against the forces wishing to maintain the present pattern of neighborhood schools, whether or not this results in de facto segregation. Present efforts to solve this problem are based on estimates of the readiness of a particular area to participate in integrated education. Little time and effort have been spent in evaluating various methods of preparing the community for change. Those who formulate and implement integration plans need to know what to expect and at what rate of speed they should or can proceed in transforming local school areas. One fact is clear: school officials are willing to try various methods and workable plans for integration.

POLITICAL MAPPING

The most basic step in studying the course of school integration controversies was to make a structural map identifying significant participants or leaders, their organizational bases, and their over-all objectives. This was, of course, a very complex research operation, involving a delineation of alliances and conflicts among various leaders and groups, and also pointing up the relationships between citywide institutions and groups and those that are neighborhood-based. In addition, a structural snapshot of one point in time has limited value. By means of an account of the course of various controversies in the past (at least since the first boycott when civil rights leaders developed differences in their respective tactics) we attempted to trace out the degree of stability or change in alignments between and among various leaders and groups.

The two conditions of the mapping project were met. First, the questions asked and the issues covered in the interviews and observations were carefully worked out <u>before</u> the field work began. This does not mean that the questions and issues to be covered were unalterably fixed before going into the field. On the other hand, the investigators did not rush to explore every controversy that developed, regardless of its possible implications. Second, the research procedures for a preliminary mapping of power have now been laid out.

The following questions guided the field investigations:

Interest Groups

1. What main citywide interest groups are actively involved in school integration controversies?
2. What are their professed goals?
3. What strategies and tactics do they recommend and fight for to help in resolving integration issues? What values inform the shaping of their program?
4. Whom do they represent? What is the social composition of their rank and file?
5. How long have they been active? What events or episodes triggered off their activity or were associated with changes in the level of rank-and-file involvement?

6. What is the size of their membership or following? Have there been any recent changes? Again, are such changes associated with particular events?

7. Who are the leaders of such groups?

8. With what other leaders and groups are they allied on a citywide basis?

9. What conditions seem to be associated with changes in the patterns of alliance and conflict of any one group with others?

10. Do they have linkages with particular neighborhood groups? When do such linkages form and dissolve? What conditions seem associated with this?

11. Is it possible to suggest any stages in the school integration controversy in terms of goals, tactics, strategies, alliances of citywide groups? When, for example, is there a more clearcut polarization of sides? When do we find a high degree of cohesion or cleavage within the civil rights groups, PAT groups, and others?

12. How do various opposing interest groups communicate with one another, if at all? What conditions precipitate communications?

13. What are the effects, if any, of increased or decreased communications?

Educational Bureaucracy

1. What are the lines and patterns of power in the educational bureaucracy?

2. To what extent is the Board an autonomous entity vis-a-vis the Mayor or the State Board of Education? What are some consequences of such relationships among these parties?

3. What effects, if any, do communications from various interest group leaders have on Board plans and long-range commitments? Are their policies greatly affected by boycotts, marches, and demonstrations? What policies, and in what ways?

4. Would one characterize the educational bureaucracy in New York City as a highly centralized or decentralized organization? If the latter, as is so often suggested, how much autonomy does a local school board or principal have in the running of a school? In the implementation of high level policies, does the neighborhood

9

school have a great deal of leeway or very little?

5. Where are the main centers of power in the public school system? At what levels in the chain of command? Why?

6. How does the Board reach decisions about integration policy, about specific plans? What groups most and least impinge on such decisions? How and why?

7. What accounts for the present ineffectiveness of school integration plans as measured by such indicators as continued de facto segregation, inferior schools in nonwhite ghettos, continued polarization of sides, and so forth?

8. On what issues is the Board itself united or divided? On what lines and for what reasons? How is this related to the Board's effectiveness?

9. What changes have taken place in Board outlook and specific plans over the past several months?

System Behavior

1. In terms of all these questions, is it possible to delineate any discernible stages in the school integration issue?

2. Are relationships among opposed groups more or less conducive to extreme conflict, perhaps even violence, than they were three or six months ago?

Obviously, not all the evidence on these questions could be documented in this report. Rather, this mapping operation formed the basis for suggesting where the major power centers are likely to be and therefore where the more inclusive future study would do well to focus.

There was no reason to assume at the start that a citywide focus is the best vantage point from which to study the power aspect of this issue. It might be that local school boards and principals have sufficient power to shape any higher level plans and policies to suit their own needs. Or it might be that interest groups function effectively only at the neighborhood level where people more clearly perceive their personal interests and as a result are more easily mobilized. On the other hand, the major power centers might be at the city or perhaps even the state level. There was no reason to draw artificial boundary lines and study the city as a closed system, a mistake characterizing too many community power studies, even some of the more sophisticated ones.

To repeat, the point of mapping was to suggest where to concentrate a future study. One can always argue that an inclusive power study should be concerned with all levels of the system, including in its purview more attention to the values and attitudes of the citizenry. The assumption that leaders closely represent the aspirations of the citizens seemed to need examination in large urban settings where conditions of apathy, alienation, and cynicism are believed to prevail. [1] A year of preliminary scouting and mapping has given some empirical answers to this question.

Qualitative interviews were conducted with some fifty leaders and informed citizens at the citywide and subcommunity levels. The respondents represented all shades of interests and opinion concerning integration of the public schools. Some twenty-five meetings were attended, again at both citywide and neighborhood levels.

The selection of respondents was determined largely by the established procedures from community power studies and a less structured "snowball" technique. Well-informed and co-operative respondents were asked to refer to others who either occupied positions of formal authority in the school system, were the leaders of interest groups, or were so strategically situated as to have valid information on the actual wielding of power in integration controversies.

A major objective of the political mapping was to investigate data availability and learn what data sources are valuable for a full-scale study of integration in New York City. Relevant sources include the following:

---

[1] See Appendix B, "Big City Political Systems: A Speculative Extrapolation", in Robert E. Agger, Daniel Goldrich, and Bert E. Swanson, The Rulers and the Ruled: Political Power and Impotence in American Communities (New York, John Wiley and Sons, 1964). Also see Murray Levin's study of Boston, The Alienated Voter (New York: Holt, Rinehart and Winston, Inc., 1960).

1. Board of Education statistical materials on each school, including attendance records, racial composition of schools, reading level of all children in schools, number of licensed teachers, student turnover, and so forth.

2. Materials collected by social scientists, notably those of Eleanor Sheldon and her associates at the Russell Sage Foundation, on school and neighborhood characteristics.

3. Census materials on social compostion of various neighborhoods relevant in sampling.

4. Interviews with Board personnel and others at various levels in the public school system, interest group leaders, teachers, political officials, journalists, and reporters.

5. Observations of meetings of political groups at the city level and in selected areas within the neighborhoods.

OUTLINE OF THE STUDY REPORT

Political mapping begins with a retrospective analysis of a Decade of the Integration Controversy (Chapter II). The three phases of the past decade furnish the raw materials for the Politics of Education (Chapter III). The construction of a detailed political map has two major dimensions: Direct Influence (Chapter IV) and Indirect Influence (Chapter V). The Strategies for Power (Chapter VI) are developed for both the integration forces and their opponents. Their relative effects are explored in the local subcommunity in an attempt to measure White Parent Decisions (Chapter VII) and a Factoring of Subcommunity Variables (Chapter VIII).

Chapter 2

A DECADE OF INTEGRATION CONTROVERSY IN THE PUBLIC SCHOOLS: 1954-1963

Just three weeks before the historical United States Supreme Court decision on Brown v. The Board of Education in May, 1954, the Intergroup Committee on New York's Public Schools called for a thorough investigation of the city's de facto segregated schools. Professor Kenneth Clark and others charged that educational standards were lower in predominantly Negro and Puerto Rican schools of the area and that the children "not only [felt] inferior but [were] inferior in academic achievement." These schools, Clark continued, did not have enough teachers, counseling, or guidance programs. There were too many classes for retarded children and too few for gifted pupils. Clark interpreted this condition as making it

> . . . no longer necessary to have specific techniques for gerrymandering schools and excluding Negro children from academic and other specialized high schools. . . . These children by virtue of inadequate elementary education cannot compete with other children in high school. [1]

These remarks set the stage for a decade of integration controversy in the public schools of New York City. The controversy has moved through three phases, each generally associated with the administration of one of three different Superintendents of Schools. The first was the study phase under Superintendent William Jansen from July, 1954, to August, 1958. This period was essentially one of research, discussion, and some tentative formulation of integration plans. The second was the experimental-permissive formulation of open enrollment under Superintendent John Theobald from September, 1958, to June, 1962. The third and more militant phase began with the superintendency of Calvin Gross in October, 1962. The first period emphasized desegregation of de facto segregated schools following the dictum

---

[1] The New York Times, April 25, 1954.

of the 1954 Supreme Court decision. The second period emphasized quality education. The third period concentrated on integration and its value for quality education.

PHASE I. COMMITTEES, STUDIES, AND REPORTS

The demand for an investigation had an immediate impact.
Colonel Arthur Levitt, President of the Board of Education,
asked the Public Education Association to conduct a "full, impar-
tial, and objective inquiry" into the status of public education for
Negro and Puerto Rican children "for the purpose of aiding all
concerned in the attainment of the ultimate goal: the completely
integrated school. "[1] The Association's report, submitted in
October, 1955, while clearing the School Board of charges of in-
tentionally segregating Negroes and Puerto Ricans, did find that
the populations of 71 per cent of the city's schools were composed of 90 per cent or more of one race. The report also
pointed to marked differences in the quality of education between
predominantly Negro and predominantly white public schools.
The schools serving the former group were older, teacher turnover was higher, and class sizes were larger. This report became the basis for the work of a newly formed Board of Education Commission on Integration. The Commission proceeded
according to the following principle enunciated by the Board:

> Today, education is perhaps the most important
> function of state and local government. . . . It is
> the very foundation of good citizenship. Today it is
> a principal instrument in awakening the child to cul-
> tural values, in preparing him for later professional
> training, and in helping him to adjust normally to his
> environment. In these days, it is doubtful that any
> child may reasonably be expected to succeed in life
> if he is denied the opportunity of an education. . . .
> We come then to the question presented. Does
> segregation of children in public schools solely on
> the basis of race, even though the physical facilities
> and other "tangible" factors may be equal, deprive
> the children of the minority groups of equal

---

[1]The New York Times, July 14, 1954.

14

educational opportunities? We believe that it does.

. . . To separate them from others of similar age and qualifications solely because of their race generates a feeling of inferiority as to their status in the community that may affect their hearts and minds in a way unlikely ever to be undone. . . .

We conclude that in the field of public education the doctrine of "separate but equal" has no place. Separate educational facilities are inherently unequal. [1]

During the next three years a number of reports were issued by six subcommittees on Zoning, Educational Standards and Curriculum, Guidance, Educational Stimulation and Placement, Teacher Assignments and Personnel, Community Relations and Information, and Physical Plant and Maintenance. The Commission urged three main methods of desegrating the city's schools "without abandoning the principle of the neighborhood school":

First, re-zoning is one method of achieving a substantial amount of mixing in some now segrated schools.

Second, it is possible by strategic building in the fringe areas to anticipate and in some degree to prevent the growth of future school and residential segregation.

Third, it is possible, by the quantitative and qualitative reassignment of school personnel in terms of the proportionate needs of the school populations involved, to reduce and eventually to overcome the present de facto discrimination against the minority groups. [2]

Controversy surrounded several subcommittee recommendations, even though all of them were accepted by the Board

---

[1]Statement and resolution of School Board President Arthur Levitt for appointment of a Commission with the idea of approaching more closely the socially integrated school in all localities. Board of Education minutes, December 23, 1954.

[2]Board of Education, Toward the Integration of Our Schools, p. 9.

of Education. The first issue arose over the assignment of experienced teachers to the "difficult", "subject", or Negro and Puerto Rican schools. Each year inexperienced new teachers were assigned to the difficult schools in the economically depressed areas of the city, thus further depriving the students of more capable and qualified teachers. The subcommittee recommends the assignment of teachers to difficult schools on the basis of school need rather than teacher preference. A three-year stint of duty in these problem schools also was recommended as a condition for promotion. Of course, the subcommittee also urged the hiring of additional teachers to reduce class size and to provide more supervision and special teaching. The teacher organizations vigorously and almost unanimously opposed the rotation of teachers as a measure which was too severe and would "cripple" the school system. The Catholic Teachers Association also opposed the proposed psychological testing and training of teachers for "wholesome attitudes" in human relations.

The second major controversy came over the proposed establishment of a centralized zoning unit. Decisions on what school a particular child should attend were determined largely by the field superintendent and the local school board. The new proposal would transfer responsibility for these critical decisions from local officials to the Board of Education at 110 Livingston Street in Brooklyn, thus making the questions less subject to local preferences.

Thus, for example, rezoning has been a major policy alternative for most school officials and civic leaders active in integration issues during this early phase. They struggled to formulate criteria for plans that would simultaneously promote integration and meet a number of educational needs, for example, those relating to continuity of instruction, space utilization, distance, hazards, and transportation. Rezoning continues to play a significant role in all recent integration plans as well.

Many of the arguments used during this period would be repeated throughout the next decade--the importance of preserving the neighborhood school, transportation and safety problems involved in sending young pupils longer distances, integrating only in the context of utilization consideration, the desirability of homogeneous (along IQ, class, and racial lines) classrooms, more specifically the effect of racially mixed classrooms on the

educational opportunities and performance levels of advanced
pupils.

PHASE II. EXPERIMENTAL-PERMISSIVE ATTEMPTS

But study recommendations require concrete programs and
techniques if they are to change the educational practices of a de
facto segregated system. In a large-scale organization with some
45,000 teachers and supervisors and a million students, the
formulation of specific programs, strategies, and tactics is necessary to achieve the ideal of equal educational opportunities
sought by this northern city. Eventually these would be worked
out in bureaucratic terms within administrative channels. The
subcommittee reports and recommendations now were turned
over to the School Board staff to spell out the details. This staff,
however, was hardly prepared for such a complex task. Many
educational principles were subject to serious scrutiny, if not
caught up in some lack of logic which only confused those who demanded the change. Educational policy in one period appeared to
contradict that of another period. For a number of generations
school officials had believed, advocated, and maintained the
neighborhood school concept. They had exhorted the teachers to
play prominent roles in school-community relations and encouraged parents to become involved in the schools attended by their
children in their local neighborhoods. If these policies created
de facto segregated schools, then the situation was caused not by
the educators but by the individual decisions of citizens when they
bought or rented their homes in the neighborhoods of their choice.

There was little clear understanding on the part of educators of the major questions raised by the committee reports,
other than the provision of equal educational opportunity for all
children, regardless of race, creed, or national origin. Who in
New York City could quarrel with this objective? But each administrative move to change specific policies affecting the education of Negroes and Puerto Ricans ran into trouble. There was
prgmatic concern to do something in response to the demands of
the Negro spokesmen of the NAACP, the Urban League, and of
other liberal groups such as Americans for Democratic Action
and the Anti-Defamation League. At the same time, however,
the administrators were trying to effect major changes in a system with narrow constraints and scant financial resources. The
people making the demands had little real power over those who

decided matters at City Hall. Once the recommendations were made, the school administrators were in a position to decide what specific plans to implement.

After lengthy internal planning some small-scale, essentially experimental programs were evolved by Superintendent John Theobald. All these programs were voluntary in nature as Theobald, a politically adept former Deputy Mayor and confidant of Mayor Robert F. Wagner, began to innovate. Rather than establish a teacher rotation program to move experienced teachers into the difficult schools, he asked for volunteers. Twenty-five teachers offered to serve in the some 1,400 positions in difficult schools. This failure to attract teachers voluntarily also doomed the rotation plan. A second innovation was the experimental Higher Horizons program, designed to raise the cultural and achievement aspirations of students from economically depressed areas. The third experiment was the open enrollment program whereby minority children could petition to attend underutilized white schools.

Most participants and observers agreed that not enough minority children volunteered, nor did the program check the growth of predominantly minority group schools. For example, in the fall of 1962, 118 elementary schools had 90 per cent or more Negro and Puerto Rican enrollments as compared with 94 in the fall of 1960; 29 junior high schools had 85 per cent or higher Negro and Puerto Rican enrollments as compared with 22 in the fall of 1960. This trend toward increasing numbers of minority group schools was due partly to the continued increase and residential segregation of the Negro and Puerto Rican populations.

It is important to view the open enrollment program in a political context. In 1960 Rev. Milton Galamison and some associates seceded from the NAACP because they were discouraged about its political role and that of the Urban League. They formed their own group, the Parents' Workshop for Equality. They organized a number of civil rights leaders from the NAACP and the Urban League, as well as parents from all five boroughs, especially Brooklyn, and threatened a strike in the ghetto schools. Although the strike did not materialize, many civil rights and other leaders, including education officials, agreed that the open enrollment program was at least in part a response to the pressure of the threat. As one militant integrationist put it: "The

18

Board had never acted after all the academic discussion, data, and moral argument. Many times we would all have agreement that something should be done; but when it finally came to moving the children, they wouldn't do it. "

The actual Open Enrollment program was carried out not so much under the publicly stated guise of achieving greater racial balance but rather to "redistribute pupils between over- and under-utilized schools. " It was legitimated to the wider community, then, more on the basis of improving school-plant utilization than for purposes of racial balance. The success of the program depended on a number of factors--the extent of preparation of receiving schools, teachers, parents, and students, the extent to which such remedial services as guidance counselors and reading help were provided, the extent of segregation in the receiving schools, and so forth. [1] One of these other factors was obviously the number of minority children affected. By 1963 civil rights and other civic leaders decided that not enough children had been affected or were likely to be either in the very near or distant future. The term <u>experimental voluntarism</u> perhaps best describes the open enrollment program and this phase in a decade of integration.

Perhaps the most important aspect of the Theobald administration was the creation of the Black Cabinet, an informal advisory group of Negroes from the civil rights movement. For the first time the Negro civil rights groups had direct access to the authorities governing the school system. They were no longer dependent on traditional, but white, civil rights and liberal organizations. Now they could express their demands directly.

Theobald had learned his political lessons well while in City Hall. He was also responding to a series of challenges offered by Negro attorney Paul Zuber, who in 1958 organized the "Harlem Nine," a group who withdrew their children from the schools, claiming that such schools were inferior and that the Negro had a right to equal education immediately. This was the first time a specific strike technique had been used in the civil

---

[1]For a survey of the attitudes of "receiving" parents see Bert E. Swanson and Clare Montgomery, "White Citizen Response to the Open Enrollment Program," <u>Integrated Education</u>, Vol. II, No. 4, August-September, 1964, pp. 44-48.

rights struggle in New York City in connection with school integration. Zuber's group opened its own school, was taken to the courts by the Board of Education, and lost the case on the grounds that the substitute facility was inferior. The decision was rendered on rather complicated legal grounds to the effect that New York City is obliged to provide equal teaching services for all schools and that judgment in such cases is partly under the jurisdiction of the court, since teachers are servants of the state.

On another occasion, however, Zuber won his case and the integration of New York schools began in earnest when the Skipwith case, referred to in Chapter I, was decided in favor of Negro parents who withdrew their children in protest against the inferior racially segregated schools.

PHASE III. MILITANCY AND BIPOLARIZATION

Three events marked the beginning of the next phase of increasing militancy and pressure from the civil rights groups and a concomitant bipolarization of the dispute as white PAT citizens organized a counterboycott. First, in June, 1963, State Commissioner of Education Allen requested all school boards throughout the state to report the racial composition in their schools. If a school did not meet the 50-50 standard for racial balance that he had established, he requested a statement of plans, if any, for redressing the imbalance. It is important to note that these were requests, not orders. The second event was the wholesale resignation of the entire Board of Education in the midst of the mayoralty election of 1961. Superintendent Theobald left soon after, and his resignation was followed by the appointment of the first non-New Yorker, Calvin Gross, to the position of Superintendent in the city's history. Third was the formation in August, 1963, of the five major civil rights groups (NAACP, Urban League, CORE, Harlem Parents' Committee, and Parents' Workshop for Equality) into a single group, the Citywide Committee for Integrated Schools, to coordinate their efforts in pressing the Board of Education for an immediate response to Commissioner Allen's requests. Galamison was designated chairman of the group and soon was directing it not as a coordinating organization but as a separate entity. As he began to announce actions on his own, without consulting the member organizations, they all withdrew. The Citywide Committee remains in existence but now has no constituency. This was an important development, symbolizing a very basic split in outlook, strategy, and tactics within the civil rights camp that will continue to affect the course of any future integration plans in the city.

This period, perhaps appropriately labeled the increased militancy stage, may be reported briefly in terms of a few major organized actions that indicate the stepped-up pace of citizen demands on the Board for integration and, most recently, for a slowdown of its integration plans. The period dramatizes the nature of the reactions of the Board and community interest groups to one another. Each has been responding to the other in rapid-fire fashion, at least in comparison to the previous phase. The nature and timing of the Board's integration plans on the one hand and of the community's demands to speed up or slow down integration on the other must be understood in terms of such an action-reaction perspective.

The New York City Board of Education reported back to State Commissioner Allen with the Plan for Integration, referred to in Chapter I.

The Citywide Committee for Integrated Schools, mainly a Negro civil rights organization, was thoroughly dissatisfied with the Plan. Rev. Milton Galamison threatened to boycott the schools in September unless the Board of Education developed a broader plan with a specific time table for implementing it. The boycott was called off temporarily upon receipt of a signed agreement that the Board of Education would provide by December 1 a tentative report and plan with a specific schedule for accomplishing the integration of the city's schools. The Board promised to consult with civil rights and other interested groups and to submit a final plan by February, 1964. These final plans would include "provisions for a substantial, realistic and working program of integration in every school district in September, 1964."

The December Interim Report [1] was no more satisfactory than the first one, even though the checklist on the progress and accomplishments of specific programs was attempted. This time, however, the civil rights groups staged a picket and sit-in

_____

[1] Board of Education of the City of New York, Progress Toward Integration (September 1-November 30, 1963) and Plans for the Immediate Future, December 3, 1963.

at some schools and began to plan a major boycott of the schools in February. The Board of Education was quick to present very specific plans before the boycott in the hope that it would be called off. [1] The major proposal was the establishment of common zones (Princeton Plan pairing) for elementary schools with substantially different ethnic composition. The greatest distance traveled by a student would not exceed two and one-half miles nor thirty minutes in travel time. Such selected additional educational benefits would be given these paired schools as smaller class size, more teachers, special services, and so forth. Twenty of the 134 elementary schools whose percentage of minority group pupils was 90 or more met the criteria and were designated for pairing with 20 white schools.

But this time the civil rights groups refused to postpone their boycott plans. On February 3 they succeeded in keeping almost a half-million students home. However, Board of Education President James Donovan labeled the boycott a "fizzle" and refused to be intimidated or influenced by the size of the turnout. Such an adamant attitude stimulated Rev. Galamison to call for a second boycott late in the spring of 1964.

However, many civil rights groups opposed him, especially those with national organizations, such as the NAACP, the Urban League, and CORE. Some local CORE groups lent support, overruling a directive from James Farmer in the national office. They could do so more readily than the NAACP or the Urban League, since they had been formed on a much more federated basis with local chapters having more autonomy. Roy Wilkins expressed the view shared by many in the white reform groups as well as the civil rights organizations when he said, "We should let the children go to school while the adults argue." Farmer had a different rationale for his opposition. He was concerned in an election year with a reaction from the white community when they went to the polls.

Three demonstrations took place in rapid succession in March. The Puerto Rican community was first with its Sunday, March 1, pro-integration parade at City Hall. Two thousand

---

[1] Board of Education, Better Education Through Integration.

persons called for emphasis on the Spanish language, more Puerto Rican school officials, and reorganization of the vocational schools. On March 13 some 15,000 whites under the leadership of the Parents and Taxpayers League (PAT) paraded before City Hall in defense of the neighborhood schools and in opposition to Princeton Plan pairings and compulsory busing of children. The second Negro boycott came three days later, when some 268,000 children stayed away from school (school officials estimate that 100,000 or 10 per cent normally are absent).

These displays of strength soon were followed by a visit from State Commissioner Allen in April, when he gave informal encouragement to civil rights groups and assumed the responsibility of providing a report (now called the Allen Report) by May.[1] In the eyes of civil rights leaders this study suggested basic structural reforms in the school system that would increase integration: a 4-4-4 grade plan and educational complexes. The report united civil rights groups once more. Galamison welcomed it as a "forceful, extremely imaginative approach, a giant step in the right direction," and the NAACP called it a "model for every northern city."

On May 18 some 5,000 persons participated in a March for Democratic Schools sponsored by the NAACP and organized by Bayard Rustin in support of the recommendations of the Allen Report. The march was attended by only one-third of the total number they had sought.

Within two weeks Superintendent Gross made public two study reports that set the schools' integration policy for the coming year, 1964-1965. The first was a two-week study by the Joint Planning Committee for More Effective Schools,[2] which was given the mission of helping the Superintendent to develop "a new design for quality education." The members represented three levels of the bureaucracy--the Superintendent's staff, the Council of Supervisory Associations, and the United Federation of Teachers.

---

[1] The State Education Commissioner's Advisory Committee on Human Relations and Community Tensions, Desegrating the Public Schools of New York City, May 12, 1964.

[2] New York City Public Schools, Report of Joint Planning Committee for More Effective Schools to the Superintendent of Schools, May 15, 1964.

Essentially they proposed prekindergarten classes for ages 3-4, heterogeneous classes, team teaching, nongraded blocs, more teaching resources, coordination with other city agencies, maximum utilization of the school plant, and the establishment of a community relations expert in each school. They urged that these proposals be instituted in the schools in September.

The major and final integration report[1] was published as school was about to close and was to be implemented in September with little reference to the Allen Report. Superintendent Gross's three major programs won few accolades and much opposition. The first and most controversial was community zoning, or the pairing of three white schools with four predominantly minority schools, instead of the 20 schools proposed earlier. One limited pairing of one grade only was added later. The second program transferred eighth-grade pupils from 10 junior high schools to 33 senior high schools. Sixth graders in 44 elementary schools would be transferred to junior high schools. The third program changed the feeder patterns of junior high schools.

The plan was attacked from all sides. PAT called it a violation of the neighborhood school principle. The Negro civil rights groups were dissatisfied. Galamison charged that it was "little more than a reshuffling of some Negro children to other segregated schools." Some teachers were concerned with the administrative and status implications of transferring students in and out of the junior high schools. After two weeks of negotiation the civil rights groups gained a modification of the transfer plan which would increase the amount of integration.

The final character of the plan served to unite civil rights groups, all of whom were strongly opposed. They insisted on a series of meetings to discuss future plans for 1965. These would focus on such topics as the capital budget, site selection for new school construction, the educational park, and integration of junior and senior high schools. In May civil rights leaders agreed with Superintendent Gross to call a moratorium on demonstrations, boycotts, or strikes of any kind, as well as on demands for increased integration in 1964-1965, if he would agree to work out with them over a period of many months a series of plans for a broad-scale integration program to be set in motion in September,

---

[1] Board of Education of the City of New York, Action Toward Quality Integrated Education, New York, May 28, 1964.

1965. Those meetings proceeded on a tenuous basis. From time
to time one civil rights group or another withdrew from the meetings, or the whole pro-integration group boycotted because it felt
that no progress was being made or because the members refused
to sit with the opposition.

At the same time the opposition group (Parents and Taxpayers) stepped up its attack on the Board and its integration program
for September, 1964. A special target was the Princeton Plan
pairings, scheduled for four instead of 20 local areas. Despite its
defeat in the courts, in local and citywide Board of Education hearings, in meetings with the Superintendent, in the City Council, at
City Hall, and in the State Legislature, PAT threatened and finally staged its own boycott in the opening days of school, September
13 and 14, 1964. They succeeded in turning out some 275,000
students, roughly the same number as the second Negro boycott.
This show of strength led Mayor Wagner to believe that PAT represented a large enough segment of white parents to merit equal participation with civil rights and moderate groups in meetings with
Dr. Gross and his staff. He thus legitimized their position in the
controversy, which up to that time had been in doubt. Then there
were two sets of meetings with school officials. One was the series
with civil rights leaders that had been going on all summer. The
second covered the broad spectrum of interested educational groups
who discussed and evaluated past programs and such future plans
as the educational park.

Meanwhile Rev. Galamison, the militant integrationist,
expressed his extreme dissatisfaction not only with the 1964 integration plans but also with the outcome of the meetings of civil
rights leaders with Dr. Gross and his staff. Galamison organized
a long-term shut-down of segregated junior high schools and
special 600 schools for delinquent and retarded children. This
boycott lasted for about a month and was called off following the
abrupt dismissal of Superintendent Gross in the spring of 1965.
He also demanded the immediate promotion of at least 200 Negroes
and Puerto Ricans into supervisory positions in the school system.

Once more there was a basic split within the civil rights coalition, with two different perspectives and strategies moving in
direct opposition. The established, traditional, nationally oriented
civil rights groups (NAACP, Urban League) favor continued political bargaining. They have limited contact with or appeal for the
Negro proletariat in Harlem or Bedford-Stuyvesant. The more

grassroots, locally oriented civil rights groups (Parents' Workshop for Equality, Harlem Parents, some CORE chapters) favor direct action. They claim that after a decade of bargaining and dialogue little integration has been affected and little is likely to result in the future from the initiative of the Superintendent or the Board of Education unless they are pushed by a broadly based coalition in the community.

The degree to which broad coalition pressure on the Board of Education, the Superintendent, and the Mayor may result in speedier and more encompassing integration efforts depends on the future alliances and commitments of the many moderate groups in the city. These include citywide professional organizations concerned with education or children (Public Education Association, Citizens' Committee for Children), traditional social reform oriented civil organizations (American Jewish Congress, Anti-Defamation League, American Jewish Committee, Civil Liberties Union, Anti-Defamation League, American Jewish Committee, Civil Liberties Union, Protestant Council, Catholic Interracial Council), and liberal political groups (Liberal Party, Americans for Democratic Action, Reform Democrat clubs), and parents groups (United Parents Association). A coalition of these large moderate groups may well hold the balance of power on the integration issue. The direction in which they move--and they are by no means a monolithic force--certainly will affect the political strategy and strength of both integration and opposition groups as each attempts to influence the course of integration in the future.

Many civil rights leaders feel that a leadership vacuum exists in New York City with regard to integration issues. The absence was demonstrated most dramatically during 1964-1965. A number of moderate groups strongly criticized some of the Board's integration plans. Some supported limited plans that the Board itself later abandoned or modified. One such group, the United Parents' Association, came out against the opposition boycott only at the last minute. This illustrates a more general point, that the ability of an organization to take a position and act quickly in periods of crises is very much affected by its structure, especially by the nature and degree of constituency pressures. Indeed, any positions and alliances taken by an organization are affected by such considerations. This is one explanation for the recurring splits between the NAACP and the

Urban League, whose leaders must go through structured channels before taking positions on local New York City issues, and a grassroots organization led by a charismatic leader, such as the Harlem Parents' Association or the Parents' Workshop for Equality, and having no large organization base or constituency to hold it accountable.

CONCLUSION

This brief historical sketch makes it clear that (1) one cannot understand the course of school integration plans and controversies in New York City without constant reference to the exercise of power and influence within, between, and among the various interested parties to the issue; (2) the struggle for quality integrated education becomes a split issue, with some groups emphasizing quality and others integration; and (3) the situation in New York City is one of considerable flux and crisis. It is in just such a critical period that the outlooks and strategies of various groups are most visibly expressed and most amenable to study. Here is a unique opportunity to study and understand the social forces that affect the course of events.

Chapter 3

THE POLITICS OF EDUCATION

INTRODUCTION

In order to understand the community contention, controversy, and conflict surrounding school desegregation and integration, one must view the recent events in New York City as a political system at work. All the attributes of politics save the political party labels of Democrat and Republican are manifest in the disputes over how the public schools shall provide equal opportunity for all. The school system has a very specific geographic jurisdiction and constituency, as well as a legal character which spells out its purpose and determines who shall govern. It has the responsibility and authority to make the specific decisions that guide the day-to-day administration of education in the classroom.

Furthermore, there is substantial disagreement on virtually every aspect of public education. Many differences of opinion have been expressed on the subject of American education, how much money should be spent, the doctrines and values disseminated in the curriculum, who shall govern the school system, and many other important issues. These differences arise between expert educators and laymen representing the parents and the community, between taxpayers and school officials, between teachers and administrators, and between the conservative and the more liberal forces in the community. The dynamics of these expressed differences can best be described as a political process in which the highly motivated gave little credence to those with competing claims.

Certainly the efforts to bring about a racial balance of American schools has become a major political issue in many communities throughout the country. The political struggle for the past decade to desegregate the schools of the South is no longer a battle over the constitutional doctrine of "separate but equal" but a quarrel over states' rights. In the North, on the other hand, the issue revolves around the value of integration and the choice of methods to provide equality of opportunity as well as an enriching educational experience. In both settings the contestants have vigorously pursued their points of view and generated a politics best described by E. E. Schattschneider as socialization of conflict.[1]

Two sets of scholars have converged in their attempts to define decision-making about public education as a political process. The first is a small but growing number of research-oriented educators who, for example, have met as a task force to discuss "The School as a Political Institution" under the auspices of The University Council for Educational Administration. The second group, political scientists, also small in number, have turned their attention to education as the agency of local government which consumes the largest public expenditure.

On occasion these scholars have combined their efforts and met to discuss political decisions, policies, and programs in the educational arena. A recent seminar on the "Processes of Community Decision-Making and Change and Their Influence on Education" has resulted in a published report entitled The Politics of Education.[2] These participants, clearly recognizing the political value of the educational system, discussed the acquisition, maintenance, and use of power by those who wish to influence the conduct of our public schools.

However, the traditional point of view of most educators is that the school is autonomous. This concept has been the most pervasive doctrine in education. Autonomy in this case has two dimensions. The first is the geographic factor of localism and the belief that the control over school policy is centered in the autonomous local community, where the school is established, operated, and maintained. Here, too, the educational values and policies are determined, reflecting local needs and sentiments. The New England child may be given a different education than his contemporary in the South or the West. The suburban child receives a different education than the urban one. In fact, the resistance to consolidation of schools in the suburbs represents differences of values and also insistence of local citizens that

---

[1]For an interesting discussion and description of the contagion of conflict, see E. E. Schattschneider, The Semi-Sovereign People: A Realist's View of Democracy in America (New York: Holt, Rinehart and Winston, 1960, p. 39.

[2]Robert S. Cahill and Stephen P. Hencley, The Politics of Education in the Local Community (Danville, Ill.: The Interstate Printers and Publishers, Inc.), 1964.

they retain the power to participate in educational decisions. But contemporary events have made this concept obsolete and unrealistic, since below the surface of any school system one finds that the locality is very dependent on a series of external forces, such as financial and educational standards. To be sure, the local school system is one of the last aspects of local function to attract the attention of the federal government, as, for instance, in the form of federal aid to education. Federal aid will have been preceded by such substantial impact on local behavior as the rulings of federal courts on the practice of local schools to allow release time for religious education and on the civil rights of Negroes in segregated schools.

The second dimension of autonomy in the schools is the fact that while American education is essentially a public responsibility, it is apolitical in nature and is the subject of many competing and contradictory expectations and demands. The schools serve as an instrument for those who seek, for example, the particular social objectives of a racially integrated society. On the whole, educators prefer to exclude politics from school affairs. By setting up separate districts they have succeeded in keeping schools outside the reach of spoils politics normally associated with partisan politics. In setting up separate special school districts and holding nonpartisan elections for school board officials, the educators have artificially and superficially removed the schools from the essential political decisions that must be made. Their narrow view of politics, mostly in terms of partisan labels, ignores the basic issue of realistically assessing their own political roles. For example, by using political partisanship as a measure, Neal Gross found that the greater the political activity of school board members, "the less likely they were to have had 'good' reasons for running for the school board."[1] Recent studies, however, have tended to emphasize the politics of education in the broader sense of negotiation and bargaining. Educator Ralph Kimbrough believes that the question has become "one of how the educational leader can be most effective in the politics of education."[2] The Syracuse group of political scientists agrees

---

[1]Neal Gross, Who Runs Our Schools? (New York: John Wiley and Sons, 1958), p. 82.

[2]Ralph Kimbrough, Political Power and Educational Decision-Making (Chicago: Rand McNally, 1964), p. 275.

that the future of public education will be "determined by those who can translate public need into public policy--by schoolmen in politics."[1]

Thus, while the doctrine of autonomy--from both extracommunity linkages and internal community politics--persists among educational leaders, contemporary practice suggests a far different set of relationships. This is not to say that some school systems are not more autonomous than others, but clearly the large urban systems are highly dependent upon the political forces that sustain and utilize them. New York City receives substantial state and federal aid, about one-third of its operating budget. It has also requested an enormous billion-and-one-half dollar appropriation from the federal government for a crash education program in the depressed areas of the city. The State of New York has established specific educational standards for the quality of teachers, curricula, libraries, and student achievement through the Board of Regents examination.[2] Even the bureaucratic staff responds to educational values from outside the community. The recent Superintendent came from Pittsburg and was educated elsewhere. The public school system also is related to the local private and parochial schools, as well as to the suburban public school systems which many families have selected in preference to the city's schools.

If the local autonomy of the school is illusory, then how can it be better understood as part of a larger and more complex labyrinth of political forces involving the legal authority of government? Political scientists traditionally view the school as a part of the local government, for which they construct a hierarchical framework depicted by a pyramid of layers with the federal units at the apex and the local units at the base. Each level of government has been assigned, explicitly or implicitly, a specific jurisdiction in the management of public affairs. These

[1]Stephen K. Baily, R. T. Frost, P. E. Marsh, and R. C. Wood, Schoolmen and Politics: A Study of State Aid to Education in the Northeast (Syracuse, N.Y.: Syracuse University Press, 1962),p. 108.

[2]Board of Education of the City of New York, A Five-Year Crash Program for Quality Education: An Attack on Unemployment and Poverty Through Improved Educational Opportunity, (New York: October 22, 1964).

jurisdictions areal or geographic in nature. There are, for example, 17,800 municipalities and some 45,000 school districts in the United States.

But the concept of levels or layers of government does not explain the day-to-day operational relationships--administrative and political--which in fact are substantially intertwined all at the same level where the public problem or program is located. Luther Gulick suggests that we view the federal constitutional system as "made up of partially autonomous governmental structures which differ primarily with respect to the extent of the constituencies and boundaries on which they rest."[1] We have, therefore, three extensions of government: federal (one unit), state (50 units), and local (100,000 units). Each may or must participate in selected ways on selected aspects of public functions.

URBAN EDUCATION

Educators have begun to differentiate between the character of American school districts. Luvern Cunningham emphasizes the need to classify the 45,000 school districts. He proposes a taxonomy with the following variables:

1. Degree of discretion available to the local school board;
2. financial support pattern;
3. geography;
4. index of population and nucleation;
5. method of school board selection;
6. bureaucratization of the school organization;
7. socio-economic characteristics of the district's adult population;
8. measure of transiency among the adult population;
9. leadership style of the chief school officer;
10. decision-making behavior of the local school board;
11. posture of the mass media;

---

[1]Luther Gulick, The Metropolitan Problem and American Ideas (New York: Alfred Knopf, 1952), p. 30.

12. posture of the district's special interest groups toward education;
13. stance of religious groups toward the public schools. [1]

Response to the rapid urbanization of America is slow, but there is a growing recognition that the three types of population aggregates--central city, suburban, and rural--require three quite different kinds of schools. John A. Bartky, for example, states that:

> The school system of the large city is extensive and involved, and the size of the community permits school government that is likely to be politically dominated and influenced by pressure groups; the suburban school, which usually emphasizes curriculum content, is particularly susceptible to excessive lay participation in control; and the rural school can become the victim of local power interest. [2]

The problems of the city are essentially organizational, involving, as they do, large numbers of students with individual differences. In the suburbs the problem again is organizational, the need to meet broad educational needs at minimum costs.

Still, most educational concepts come from our rural experience. Greater emphasis must be given to the complex dynamics of urbanism if we are to understand the special needs of the urban school. [3] We are beginning to recognize the special educational problems of big cities. Racial imbalance and integration must be dealt with concurrently with such other problems as improving the quality of education in the slum or depressed area schools, providing the necessary financial resources to meet

---

[1] Luvern L. Cunningham, "Community Power: Implications for Education," in Cahill and Hencley, op. cit., p. 45.

[2] John A. Bartky, Social Issues in Public Education (Boston: Houghton Mifflin Co., 1963), pp. 209-210.

[3] See B. J. Chandler, Lindley J. Stiles, and John I. Ritsuse, Education in Urban Society (New York: Dodd, Mead, and Company, 1962) and August Kerber and Barbara Bommarito, The Schools and the Urban Crisis (New York: Holt, Rinehart, and Winston (1965).

sharply rising costs, finding adequate teachers for disadvantaged children, and developing the machinery for democratic decision-making.

The democratic beliefs and concepts of Americans are changing as the country becomes transformed from a rural to an urban society. One result of this transformation is the decreasing sense of political power or lack of influence on those policies that affect our personal lives, such as where and under what conditions our children shall be educated. Urban school systems have effectively challenged our uncomplicated notion of a small group of civic leaders without political ties who decide what is good educational practice. Three major issues that have arisen make these notions obsolete and pose a real problem for those parents who wish to participate in formulating educational policies.

The first issue is the increasing prominence of the educational expert, who is professionally trained and now plays a conspicuous role in school systems across the country. We have grown to depend, if indeed we have not become too dependent, upon his judgment and his articulation of educational values and principles. The second issue is the tendency to treat most decisions in administrative terms, basing alternatives on technical criteria, rather than on the more subjective expressions of educational needs. The third, centralization of decision-making, follows from the other two, for the expert is trained and tends to prefer to base his judgments on technical grounds and hold the power close at hand in his headquarters.

Recent tendencies reveal these issues to be very much alive in New York. Superintendent Calvin Gross personified the professional armed with the best educational principles. Apparently New Yorkers agreed with neither his principles nor his administrative performance. Certainly a good deal of the early determination of which schools would participate in pairing was based on the technical criteria of travel distances, racial balance, and available building facilities. But these criteria were also subject to the test of political feasibility, both at central headquarters, where there must be sufficient authority to run the largest school system in the country, and in the local school arena, where the children and their parents are affected.

In New York City education has become the largest single item budgeted for the many functions of local government. It comprises nearly one-third of the city's three-billion-dollar budget and covers the largest number of public employees (over 40,000 teachers and more school administrators than in all of France). It also has the largest single clientele in the city government-- over one million students. Formulating and administering policy for this enormous activity becomes complex because the school system is a public agency serving the needs of an essentially democratic society. The administrators are subject to the many competing and conflicting sets of divergent demands within the metropolis. At the same time they must respond to local neighborhood and community interests. For example, in a political system which operates on the principle of scarcity, the competition for a special program for the gifted student draws away resources from slow learners. On the other hand, school leaders, policymakers, and administrators are involved in the complicated task of enhancing organizational effectiveness. Decisions made at the top of the bureaucratic structure require implementation at the lower levels. Such conflicts have subjected the New York school system to many crisis situations in the past several years.

New York City has long fulfilled its historic role as the great melting pot[1] by accommodating waves of foreign immigrants to America. Today, together with most other big cities, it is engaged in assimilating our most recent newcomers to the conditions of urban life--Negroes and Puerto Ricans. This new wave differs, however, from immigrants of the past who rapidly developed their own ethnic organizations, which political party machines were willing and able to help. Recent newcomers are United States citizens who have been led to expect all the rights and privileges of citizenship and make considerable demands on governmental services. The public school traditionally has been the principal agent in coping with the manifest and expressed differences between immigrant and old Yankee; Protestant, Catholic, and Jew; the lower and middle classes; and the other competing segments of a changing American society. Now the public school is expected to play a major part in providing the training and skills to insure equal opportunities for the latest newcomers.

---

[1] For a challenging discussion of the melting-pot concept as used for New York City, see Nathan Glazer and Daniel Moynihan, Beyond the Melting Pot: The Negroes, Puerto Ricans, Jews, Italians, and Irish of New York City (Cambridge: The M.I.T. Press and Harvard University Press, 1963).

Educational leaders in the large urban centers of the North find it difficult to fulfill the role of assimilator for Negroes and Puerto Ricans because of various forms of segregation. Residential segregation in a great metropolis produces de facto segregated schools when the neighborhood school policy is adopted and maintained. Moreover, the latest resistance to contact with and acceptance of Negroes by whites has encouraged social and psychological distance factors which inhibit, slow down, and often prohibit the ability of the school to contribute to a meaningful assimilation process. Discrimination in employment frustrates one purpose of American education--to train our youth for their proper place in the labor force. Yet, the school, itself a product of a vastly inequal society, while enabling what Lloyd Warner and his colleagues believe to be

> . . . the rise of a few from lower to higher levels, still continues to serve the social system by keeping down many people who try for higher places. The teacher, the school administrator, the school board, as well as the students themselves, play roles to hold people in their places in our social structure. [1]

Two general political developments both facilitate and complicate the task of the schools of New York City in solving the problems caused by de facto segregation. First, local government has been changing from its earlier political party machine system to an administrative state with community conservation[2] as the central ideology of the political leaders. They place great value on education, equality of opportunity, and social harmony.

---

[1]W. Lloyd Warner, Robert J. Havighurst, and Martin B. Loeb, Who Shall be Educated? The Challenge of Unequal Opportunities (New York: Harper and Brothers, 1944), p. xi. See also Patricia C. Sexton, Education and Income: Inequalities of Opportunity in Our Public Schools (New York: Viking, 1961).

[2]For a full discussion of community conservationists and other ideological types operating in American communities, see Agger, Goldrich, and Swanson, op. cit., pp. 14-32.

36

Thus, the plight of the Negro, his education, housing, and employment, become the concern of the political leaders and efforts are being made to readjust governmental programs. In fact, compensatory treatment is seriously considered and has been partially implemented in the public school system.[1]

Second, the condition of urban society has seriously threatened the Jeffersonian model of citizen participation. Steps to decentralize administration and policy-making are gradually being taken in the New York City public school system as well as in other areas of local government. In the school arena both political and administrative decentralization are well under way, as evidenced by the establishment of 25 local school boards with lay memberships. In addition, the office of community coordinator has been created and assigned to each of the administrative areas of the school system. The new 1961 charter established Local Community Planning Boards for the some 87 subcommunities in the city.[2] These are to have jurisdiction over matters of local government in the local area. It is hoped that these institutional rearrangements will facilitate citizen access to the enormous bureaucratic structure and thus reverse the mass alienation and apathy permeating much of urban life.

A POLITICAL MODEL OF THE INTEGRATION CONTROVERSY

The ensuing portrayal of the social forces that affect major educational decisions is based on the concept of the inseparability of education and politics. Indeed, one cannot understand the dynamics of school integration controversies without constant reference to the exercise of power and influence. First, the massive, sprawling educational bureaucracy of New York City is itself a political entity, composed of a number of interest groups and factions with varying degrees of influence over educational policy, at either the formulation or the implementation stage. Secondly, decisions made within the education system

---

[1] Whitney M Young, Jr. "Should There be Compensation for Negroes?" The New York Times Magazine, October 6, 1963, p. 43.

[2] See Bert E. Swanson, The Concern for Community, The Scope and Authority of Community Planning Boards, and Staffing the Local Community Planning Boards (staff reports prepared for the Committee on Community Districts of the Citizens Union of New York City).

are affected by political pressures and demands from organized groups in the wider community. The demands of militant integrationists, moderate traditional educational groups, or parents' associations, to cite a few, have had a great effect on the Superintendent and the Board of Education in formulating integration policies in recent years. In fact, some critics have portrayed the Board as having had no consistent policy or long-range plans of its own on school integration and as constantly overreacting to momentary pressures from organized interest groups.

Policies regarding school integration directly touch the very pulse of the community. Some educators and even some politicians continually claim that education and politics remain distinct. In fact, some educators and politicians have even based their own conduct in the educational arena on this view. [1]

It is the ideology of many educational administrators that only technical criteria are relevant in educational decisions. Politics has no place in such matters, they contend. This technocratic point of view holds that only professional-technical criteria should govern administrative decisions and that politics and questions of social values are irrelevant. There are no value dilemmas for the administrator, since all matters of policy can be decided by criteria of efficiency.

Any policies set by the school bureaucracy, however, must be formulated in some community context with a clear-cut recognition of zones of acceptance of the citizenry, the major clients of the system. Such policies must also be considered legitimate

---

[1] Some of this may be political rhetoric which is quite prevalent in large cosmopolitan centers like New York City. Some represents a sincere, civic-minded attempt to elevate the standards of recruitment and policy-making from the political clubhouse pattern of the past when the composition of the board, for example, reflected patronage rather than educational concerns, to a more impersonal recruitment based on professional qualifications. This, then, is an example of the trend from machine to reform politics in New York City. See Theodore J. Lowi, At the Pleasure of the Mayor (New York: The Free Press of Glencoe), for an analysis of this development; see also Edward Banfield and James Q. Wilson City Politics (Cambridge: Harvard University Press and M.I.T. Press, 1963), for a more general discussion of this change in big city political styles.

by all professional educators and civil servants who are responsible for their implementation. Public resistance this past year
to the Board's integration plans and the many private attempts to
slow down the educational changes ordered by both Board and
Superintendent demonstrated the power of community groups.
Thus, broad educational policy decisions, especially those on
school integration, can be made and implemented effectively only
by mobilizing the support or, at the very least, negating the opposition of groups within the bureaucracy and interested citizens
in the wider community.

The model used in this study is based on perspectives developed from social science research on city politics. This model
is the concept of the education arena of New York City--the main
focus of our attention--as a political entity.[1] The professional
educator is not alone in making major decisions regarding educational innovations. Large segments of the community intervene
either directly or indirectly in such matters.[2] School administrators certainly do not operate in a vacuum. Their relations
with the wider community must be analyzed with some care.

Most studies of influence in America's biggest cities have
described highly fragmented and diffused power systems. Edward
Banfield has written that the Chicago area, "from a purely formal
standpoint, can hardly be said to have a government at all."[3] He
goes on to say that

> . . . Virtually nothing can be done if anyone
> opposes--and, of course everything is always op-
> posed by someone--and therefore every opponent's
> terms must always be met if there is to be action.[4]

---

[1]The term _educational arena_ is used in preference to _bureau-
cracy_ because it limits the institutional focus much less. Thus,
the arena for school integration decisions includes virtually the
whole community and outside organizations (e.g., state and federal
government) as well.

[2]See Robert Dahl's distinction between direct and indirect
influence, in his _Who Governs?_ (New Haven: Yale University Press,
1961), pp. 163-165.

[3]Edward C. Banfield, _Political Influence_ (New York: The Free
Press of Glencoe, 1961), p. 235.

[4]_Ibid._, p. 235

Essentially the same description of New York City is offered by
Wallace Sayre and Herbert Kaufman:

> New York's huge and diverse system of govern-
> ment and politics is a loose-knit and multicentered
> network in which decisions are reached by ceaseless
> bargaining and fluctuating alliances among the major
> categories of participants in each center, and in
> which the centers are partially but strikingly iso-
> lated from one another. [1]

New York City, then, has a multiplicity of decision centers.
Each center has a core group invested with formal authority to
govern and a constellation of satellite groups which seek to influence authoritative decisions. Sayre and Kaufman have completed a detailed description of five major types of contestants
for political prizes: (1) party leaders, (2) elected and appointed
public officials, (3) the organized bureaucracies, (4) nongovernmental associations, and (5) officials and agencies of other governments. The core groups centering around the general organs of
government are the Mayor, the Board of Estimate, the City
Council, and the state and federal legislators and executives. All
other participants in the political process are satellite groups.
The Board of Education acts as a satellite group when it asks the
city administration for money. On the other hand, it constitutes
a core group for the special matters pertaining to the educational
arena. The Board, in turn, has its constellation of satellite
groups which attempt to influence the quality of education.

The concept of a core and a constellation of satellites will
guide this exploratory effort to construct a political map of the
educational arena and the integration controversy. The analogy
of a solar system is used mainly to focus attention on the structure and behavior of a dynamic system in action. Care should be
taken, however, not to reify the concept or to expect the school
system to behave exactly like the solar system or to have the
same dynamics. Rather, the analogy is a heuristic device to
portray the structure of the basic elements and attributes of the
educational arena. This is the setting of a social planetarium

---

[1]Wallace Sayre and Herbert Kaufman, Governing New York City
(New York: Russell Sage Foundation, 1960), p. 716.

40

suggested by Harold Lasswell in micromodeling where "the advantages of universality, selectivity and vividness are obtainable in reference to the flow of history into the future."[1]

As the astronomer attempts to map the solar system, he also attempts to observe its order. He must identify the entities, their number, how they are grouped, and how they may be classified. He describes the size, mass, and density of each entity and its behavioral characteristics. These observations are recorded over a period of time to explain relationships between the entities and their stability or transiency.

Political mapping involves essentially the same search for meaningful decision-making patterns. The social scientist attempts to identify the major participants and discover how they form into operations groupings. He examines their numbers, resources, goals, ideologies, strategies, and tactics, and their behavioral characteristics. His observations, too, are recorded over a period of time to discern patterns of repetitive acts and the kinds of relationships between and among the participants that will explain the process of influence and power.

The Sayre and Kaufman concept of the core and satellite groups has been modified somewhat for application to the educational arena. Figure 1 shows the system with the Board of Education as the core surrounded by five major constellations, each with its own set of satellite groups: (1) the bureaucracy and its representative groups; (2) the establishment, or traditional educational interest groups; (3) the traditional intergroup relations organizations; (4) the Negro and Puerto Rican civil rights organizations; and (5) the bipolarized neighborhood groups. The first constellation shares direct influence with the Board of Education, since they are intimately involved in the day-to-day operation of the schools and actually carry out the policy directives of the Board. The other constellations have indirect influence and expend their efforts and resources to gain access to those with direct influence and inform and persuade them of their decisional preferences.

---

[1]Harold D. Lasswell, The Future of Political Science (New York: Atherton Press, 1963), p. 140.

41

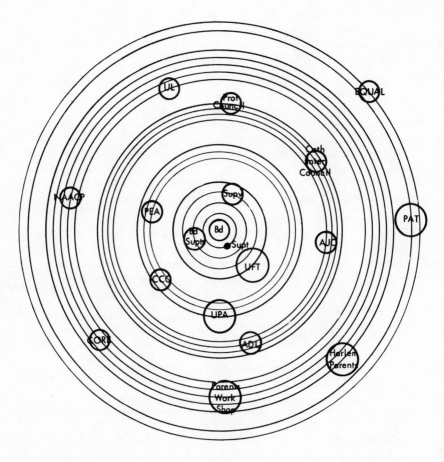

Figure I. The Core (Board of Education) and the Constellations of Satellite Groups--New York City Educational Arena, 1964.

The next three chapters will describe several factors using this conception of the educational arena. It should be stressed that these are preliminary statements based on data and estimates provided by various principal participants in the system. Since the study focuses on power relationships, these factors have a bearing on the influence of any group in the core or of any other group. The first factor is the size of groups in terms of numbers of members. The size of each group as designated on the diagram corresponds roughly to estimates provided by organizational leaders. The parents organizations, for example, are large and function as mass organizations, particularly UPA and PAT. The elite groups such as PEA are small in size. Under normal circumstances the small traditional educational groups appear to have considerable influence. A new group such as PAT has to organize mass support in order to be heard and easily prevails over EQUAL's efforts in the local neighborhood.

The second factor is distance from the core group. The bureaucracy, having direct influence, is closer than are the indirect influence community groups. The bipolarized neighborhood constellation is farthest from the core, since these groups appeared to have limited access and were considered extremists with little influence on policy. It is difficult in this preparatory study to measure precisely the influence of PAT as an opponent of pairing. Yet it is clear now that there will be few if any additional pairings in New York City.

The third factor is time. The schematic diagram is a static picture of a moment in time. Had it been drawn a year sooner (in June, 1963), there would have been no bipolarized neighborhood groups. Had it been drawn prior to the 1954 Supreme Court decision, the Negro civil rights groups would exercise little influence. A dynamic picture should show the changing power relationships as well as the shifting coalitions and alliances. The second Negro boycott, for example, found several Negro civil rights groups opposing or tacitly disapproving. Thus, a change in structure (decentralization), rules (the 1954 Supreme Court decision), or personnel (discharge of Superintendent Gross), all occurring along the time dimension, affect power relations in the educational arena.

Chapter 4

DIRECT INFLUENCE: THE CONTEST
FOR POWER AT THE CENTER

THE SCHOOL BOARD AND THE SUPERINTENDENT

The Board of Education is the formal center of authority in the educational arena. The nine-member board is appointed by the Mayor for overlapping seven-year terms. The members represent many of the diverse interests in New York City, such as a geographic allocation between the five boroughs. The most prominent concern in their appointments, however, has been to achieve ethnic balance among Protestants, Catholics, and Jews as well as among Irish, Italians, and Negroes. Theodore J. Lowi states that "The Board of Education is a dramatic example of the development of ethno-religious politics in the city."[1]

In 1961 the procedures for selecting board members was reformed after the unprecedented action of the New York State Legislature, which, meeting in special session, voted overwhelmingly to oust the entire Board. This action followed the revelation of state investigators into a scandal of school maintenance and repair. The new selection procedure allows the Mayor to continue to appoint board members, but his choice is restricted to a list of names submitted by a statutory screening panel composed of the heads of eleven citywide educational, civic, and labor organizations.

The present Board comprises top talent from New York's business and civic community. For example, the president, James Donovan, is a Wall Street lawyer, former senatorial candidate, and internationally famous for his role in the release of U-2 pilot Francis Powers from Russia. Vice-President Lloyd Garrison is a lawyer associated with the law firm of which Adlai Stevenson was a member. The board members serve in a part-time, unpaid capacity. Most of their business is conducted by five standing committees: Finance and Budget, Buildings and Sites, Law, Instructional Affairs, and Retirement. They not only hold meetings as a board but they also hold public hearings.

---

[1]Theodore J. Lowi, op. cit., p. 33.

They appoint the Superintendent and confirm all other school personnel that he nominates.

All school policy must be adopted formally by the Board. In theory the Board is entrusted to set basic educational policy which the Superintendent, the chief executive officer, implements through a large bureaucratic staff. In practice, however, the policy-administration dichotomy is false. Luther Gulick has emphasized "discretion" as the determiner of policy, adding that the administrator's "every act is a seamless web of discretion and action."[1] In fact, as the top-ranking professional educator in the system, the Superintendent has substantial policy-making powers. Naturally there is conflict between Board and Superintendent over who decides what policy shall prevail. Nonetheless, legally the Board has the final voice in deciding what integration policy to follow.

An account of a recent confrontation of the two forces will illustrate the character of the relationship between the Board and the Superintendent. In the spring of 1964, after both Superintendent Gross and the Board had undergone a long period of community harassment about school integration plans, their working relationship was reported to be near the breaking point. The Board, under the leadership of President Donovan, contended that if it was to function effectively it had to establish special committees "to deal in depth with situations as they arise." The special committees referred to were to be composed of administrative and research assistants who would evaluate the work of Dr. Gross and his assistants. They would report directly to the Board. Dr. Gross refused to accept this proposal. Through a series of informal maneuvers and meetings with State Commissioner Allen, with commissioners from other states, and with Mayor Wagner, Gross was able to defeat the plan.

This kind of critical incident typifies the division and conflict between the two parties over the many pressing and varied demands and criticisms of groups concerned with the school integration problem. As Sayre and Kaufman point out, because

---

[1]Luther Gulick, "Politics, Administration and the New Deal," chapter in The Annals (Philadelphia: The American Academy of Political and Social Science, September, 1933), p. 61.

of their visibility in the community, a core group like the Board is frequently subject to sharp community criticism. In this case the Board felt that it must proceed independently, since Gross had not yet formulated any specific plan. Having been thrust into an extremely complex system only the year before, Gross now was threatened with a teachers' strike. Smarting as they were under such public criticism, the Board members felt that Gross was vacillating, weak, failing to follow through on his plans, which had impressed them.

At times the Board itself has been quite sharply divided over the appropriate course of school integration. Though their positions have changed over time, some board members have felt compelled to move faster on integration plans in order to hold out accomplishments to Negro leaders and thereby offset a more serious mass Negro revolt against the system than occurred in the boycotts of the spring of 1964. Others feared that speedy action might well alienate many middle-class white parents and encourage them to move out of the public school system entirely. As Fred M. Hechinger of The New York Times noted:

> While some board members are still known to feel that faster integration action may be feasible, others are certain that even the present proposals will encounter serious educational obstacles and, more important, will become involved in a series of suits by white parents.
>
> This, they are afraid, will further divide the community. One board member, who has been acting as a consultant to other cities, stressed that the New York integration progress has been superior to all other urban communities.
>
> One board member is known to have threatened to prepare a minority report when the board issued its "guiding principles" last month in which the Superintendent was told in relatively specific terms what direction the final integration report was to take. The dissenting board member's objections were based on concern over intrusion on the Superintendent's administrative ground. [1]

---

[1] Fred Hechinger, The New York Times, February 6, 1964.

In brief, there seems to have been a split between moderates and liberals on the Board at certain times. It must be noted, however, that positions and coalitions change over as short a period as a few months. One position that remained in a state of flux was the struggle over the tenure of the Superintendent. Gross won his case against the Board on the committee issue. Two months later, when Donovan suffered a heart attack and withdrew, Lloyd Garrison became Acting President. Gross seemed thus to have won more control over and support from the Board.

Indeed, during the fall Gross seemed to possess the power necessary to formulate policy and expect the Board to concur. This was a striking reversal of a trend for which Max J. Rubin, a former Board President, had worked so hard. Yet in March, 1965, the Board stripped Gross of his responsibilities and placed him on leave of absence. As this is written he has formally resigned, although he will still serve in the capacity of consultant to the Board.

As of February, 1963, however, one of the main problems facing the system was:

> The line between setting general policy which
> is the Board's function, and administering the
> school system, which is the task of the professional
> staff under the direction of Dr. Gross, is being over-
> stepped. It was generally known that Max J. Rubin,
> who resigned as board chairman for reasons of
> health last December, had made the re-establish-
> ment of this clear line of separation of the board's
> priority goals. [1]

There seem to be several reasons for the Board's need periodically to reassert its power as a policy-making body. One may be that New York City still lives with the memory of the extreme corruption and scandal revealed during the Theobald administration and refuses to invest so much power in a Superintendent, lest a similar situation develop. Secondly, there may be a more general concern to prevent the development of an elitist system with so much power invested at the top, but subject to only limited constraints from the wider community.

---

[1] Ibid.

Historically, the Board rather than the Superintendent has been the target for community complaints and pressures. If the Board now were to have only a secondary role in policy-making, then this important avenue for the general citizenry to exercise influence on school integration matters would be virtually closed. This might, in turn, lead to serious alienation of some segments of the community from the school system. After all, what did Gross, an outsider, know, about the fine and delicate political balance of the New York City school system? Another reason for the Board's recurring interest in maintaining policy-making power is the natural tendency of the system toward a strong administrator. Perhaps such influentials as the Mayor and leaders of various civic groups prefer a fluid situation to ensure as much democracy as possible. Continued research must explore in some detail the dynamics of this power relation between the Superintendent and the Board.

A development that has been quite marked since June, 1964, is that the Superintendent himself assumed some of the Board's role of meeting with representatives of various civil rights and white liberal groups. Though this may have been the practice in the past, most leaders with experience in school integration controversies feel that these meetings were almost revolutionary in character. Clearly Dr. Gross had abandoned an apolitical conception of his role, feeling now that his main hope for the system lay in being able to negotiate school integration changes with such groups. He may have seen quite clearly that if the New York system was to have the strong superintendency that he obviously preferred, he must assume functions that previously the Board had carried out informally. This recent development will be discussed in a section below on citywide interest groups and their roles.

THE SUPERINTENDENCY

The competitive relationship between the Board of Education and the Superintendent of Schools over who shall decide integration policy requires much more empirical research if we are to understand the dynamics of decision-making at the very top of the school system. For the purposes of this preparatory study, however, the Board is considered the core of power and the final arbiter of major school programs. The Board must approve integration policies, and the more controversial the proposal, the more the Superintendent is inclined to have the Board play a leading role vis-a-vis the public. But it should be made clear that the Board mainly acts upon or approves proposals prepared and submitted by the Superintendent. He does so, of course, according to the guidelines and preferences laid down by the Board.

The preparation of integration proposals is not a one-man performance. The Superintendent relies heavily on a very large staff which has several specialized units devoted to integration problems. The Central Zoning Unit is responsible for ensuring maximum integration through the techniques of rezoning. It played a major role in selecting the local school areas that were paired in September, 1964. The Human Relations Unit engages in field operations to gain acceptance of integration efforts and to work with the specific problems that arise. Staff support is coordinated in the office of Assistant Superintendent in Charge of Integration Programs. The occupant of this newly created position is the principal aide to the Superintendent in formulating integration plans.

But again, just as the Board depends on the Superintendent for general integration proposals, so, too, the Superintendent depends on his administrative staff for specific details to help him choose between alternative approaches to the problem. Therefore, the concept of the superintendency characterizes the intricate network of supervisory staff drawn upon by the Superintendent. The focal point is the Board of Superintendents, a ten-member group of deputy and associate superintendents, which serves as an advisory cabinet to the Superintendent. Their influence is best described by Sayre and Kaufman.

> For more than forty years successive Boards of Superintendents have patiently instructed Superintendents in the limits of power, the risks of innovation, and the necessities of unanimity if the Superintendent is to bargain successfully with the Board of Education. In the closed world in which these ten school officials operate, each familiar with the values and aspirations of the others and accustomed to mutual accommodations, the strongest inclinations run toward minimal changes in institutional habits. [1]

---

[1] Sayre and Kaufman, op. cit., p. 281.

The day-to-day administration of the schools also is part of the superintendency. This is accomplished through a vast array of field superintendents, school-community coordinators, school principals, and their assistants. While the system is highly centralized, there have been a number of efforts to decentralize decision-making. For example, in 1961 25 local boards replaced 54 ineffective boards that had been subject to political patronage. The new boards were consulted by the Superintendent in preparing the 1964 integration program. Dr. Bernard Donovan, who has now succeeded Gross as Superintendent has just proposed the creation of 30 essentially autonomous school districts in an effort to decentralize administrative decisions. However, he has assured civil rights groups that integration policy will continue to be formulated at central headquarters in order to ensure a common citywide program. Implicit in the discussion of decentralization is the serious problem of communications between the policy makers at the top and the field administrators. The supervisory personnel have a variety of associations to represent their interests on school policy. They include the Association of the Board of Examiners, the Association of Assistant Superintendents, the High School Principals Association, the New York City Elementary School Principals Association, the Junior Principals Association, the Administrative Assistants Association (Academic High Schools), the Assistants to Principals Association, the Association of Administrative Assistants (Vocational High Schools), the Association of High School Chairmen, and others. All these associations in turn are organized into a Council of Supervisory Associations which speaks out periodically in behalf of the entire supervisory group. They are an important power group, for they carry out the policies of the Superintendent and the Board at the local school level.

Throughout the school integration debates of the past year there has been considerable opposition from school supervisors to various integration proposals of the Board and the Superintendent. Analysis of this opposition highlights some of the general features of the administrative structure that directly affect the potential effectiveness of integration plans. The supervisors claim to be very much in favor of integration but they oppose several features of earlier plans, namely pairings, extended busing, and the middle school 4-4-4 plan as presented in the Allen Report and as partially followed in the Gross plans for September, 1965. They charge that many of these proposals, rather than furthering integration, will only hasten the flight of the middle class to private and parochial schools and to the suburbs. They also feel that such integration measures will do more harm than good by failing to provide better education for all children. Their opposition has been referred to by one school official as a rebellion within the ranks. Most of the supervisors are white, and the fact that many are Jewish may activate the latent anti-Semitic feelings of some militant Negro leaders.

After the Allen Report was published, the school supervisors made a strong statement against many aspects of the plan. One group especially concerned was the Junior High School Principals Association which had been lobbying for years for pay scales commensurate with those of high school principals on the grounds that the junior high positions required equivalent skill, training, and responsibility. The middle school (grades 5-8) as proposed in the Allen plan would, of course, preclude adoption of this proposal, since the administrative level would be lowered. The resistance of these principals to integration plans was exposed by James G. Murray, President of the Junior High School Principals Association.

> The principals have no objection to conducting an educational experiment to determine the educational worth of a new program, providing planning is adequate, that there are adequate ways of protecting the youngsters and that there are provisions for evaluating the results by an impartial group.
> We do not regard this as an experiment. Right now it's just a gimmick to satisfy certain pressure groups that are more interested in a numbers game than in the education of the children. [1]

It seems obvious that various members of the supervisory staff have taken it upon themselves to redefine top level policy according to their own conceptions of what is best for the children. Many times their conceptions contradict those of the Superintendent and the Board. The educational system has undergone such change in recent years that there can be many opportunities for the supervisors to refuse to cooperate. A recent

---

[1] The New York Times, June 2, 1964.

case involving an associate superintendent suggests the lengths to which supervisory personnel can go in negating and vetoing integration plans. Such pressure and harassment was exerted on the principals and teachers within this division as to ignite another teacher uprising which was dealt with only on a temporary basis by Superintendent Gross. More will be said about this case below in the section on neighborhood variations in desegregation experience.

More general questions are raised. What of the failure in communication downward of integration plans and perhaps of many other policies? What of the apparent alienation as a result of the initial lack of influence and power in policy-making for this group? Many observers of the school system feel that communications downward have failed in the past year, at least on integration issues. One major explanation may be that the supervisory staff is known to prefer the status quo and therefore is considered likely to oppose many integration plans. The system has not yet settled sufficiently from the recent crisis of succession to have reestablished major communication channels. When he first assumed his position in June, 1963, Dr. Gross himself said: "I suspect that the most important problem I'm going to face here is communications."[1] It may be that Gross and the Board were so sensitive to the demands and pressures of civil rights groups that it seemed politically unwise to communicate with supervisory personnel until an agreement had been reached. They assumed that Negro leaders viewed the supervisors as a conservative group, the personification of a segregated school system. They also assumed that the price of the supervisors' resentment at not being included would be much less than that of alienating Negro leaders and perhaps being accused by their rank-and-file membership of compromising or at least of lacking influence at the bargaining table. According to this reasoning, it is better to have an uprising of supervisors or even teachers within the schools than to have more revolts from the Negro community. An indication of this assessment of the Negro leaders' hostility to school supervisors is found in Rev. Milton Galamison's statement after the supervisors' rebellion:

---

[1]Fred M. Hechinger, The New York Times, March 28, 1964, p. 20.

It does not surprise us that there is a sufficient number of anti-integrationists in the supervisory
ranks of the school system. The Negro and Puerto
Rican children of this city have been suffering from
the attitudes of some of these people for years.[1]

Gross may have decided that strong leadership was necessary in such crises and that he had no time for continued con-
sultation with his supervisors about various plans. Constant con-
ferring in a continually changing situation could prevent him from
getting anything done and cause his political effectiveness to
diminish. Probably all these interpretations have some bearing
on the situation. Regardless of which is most accurate, clearly
communications down the chain of command on integration matters
became limited, while the exertion of upward influence was virtually nonexistent. From the point of view of optimum effectiveness the adoption of this stratagem by the Superintendent and the
Board may have much to commend it and may involve the least
costs and most gains of any that might have been used.

THE TEACHERS

The key to any educational system is its teachers. They are,
however, seldom consulted on integration matters. Their voice
is heard mainly in the myriad of specialized and fragmented clus-
ters of teacher associations--representing grade levels (the
Elementary Teachers Association), geographic divisions (the
Brooklyn Teachers Association), and subject matter (such as
mathematics, biology, and so forth). On the whole, these organizations have not expressed themselves on integration policies.

The most powerful teachers' organization, the United Federation of Teachers, has taken a stand in support of integration.
However, the Federation has been quick to protect the teacher
from forced transfers to the difficult schools. Though it had a
very small membership only a few years ago, the New York City
UFT now claims almost 30,000 members and may well increase
to include most if not all the 42,000 public school teachers in the
near future. By now the successes of the UFT at the bargaining

---

[1]Leonard Buder, The New York Times, March 26, p. 20.

table have been well publicized across the country. They have
been instrumental in securing such reforms as more aggressive
recruitment policies, speedier publication of new eligibility lists,
higher salaries, and a centralized system of assigning substitute teachers. These reforms were hammered out in bargaining
negotiations between the UFT, the Board, and the Superintendent.
The power of the UFT in New York is highlighted by contrast
with other cities. The AFT (the American Federation of Teachers,
the parent body of the UFT) has 100,000 members throughout the
country, almost one-third of whom are in New York City.

Superintendent Gross recognized their strength and accepted their position when he indicated to a National Conference
of Professors of Educational Administration: "The UFT does
represent and will represent teachers here. We administrators
can't stick our heads in the sand and hope the union will go
away."[1] The UFT leaders are among his staunchest allies in
pushing for more school integration. They have been mobilizing
their rank and file to cooperate in integration efforts.

CONCLUSION

Much more empirical research is necessary to describe
and explain the complex relationships between and among the
Board, the Superintendent, the superintendency, and the teachers.
Sayre and Kaufman contend that

> . . . the Superintendent of Schools presides
> over but cannot lead the school system. His oppor-
> tunities for initiative are squeezed within narrow
> confines by a triangle of forces--those embodied in
> the Board of Education, in the Board of Superinten-
> dents, and in the organized teachers' groups--and
> this triangle is reinforced by the statutory details
> which the three groups, separately and together,
> have over the years succeeded in having placed in
> the State Education Law and guarded by the watch-
> ful eye of the State Department of Education. The
> isolation of the Superintendent from the Mayor does

---

[1]New York World Telegram, August 25, 1964, p. 33.

not add to the Superintendent's autonomy and leadership; instead, it helps to explain his subordination
to the triangle of forces which surrounds him. [1]

All four sets of participants play important roles in formulating integration policy. Yet the Board is in the center, for
it possesses the final legal authority to choose one alternative
over another. This decision, however, is made in the context
of the bureaucratic ritualism which characterizes New York
City's educational system and seems directly related to the
inertia and inability to respond adequately to demands for change.
The amount of rigmarole involved in the simplest requests for
information suggests an organization heavily weighted with procedures. One dramatic exchange between civil rights leaders
and Dr. Gross illustrates this problem. At the height of one of
the Jackson Heights pairing controversies an anti-integrationist
group pointed out that even if there were general acceptance of
mass busing of students, it would be impossible to accomplish,
since buses ran only east to west through the area and the schools
were located north to south. A school official was asked by a
pro-integrationist leader to write to the New York City Transit
Authority to inquire about providing a new bus route. This official, who favored the pairing, became so bogged down in rules
about clearance before even making the request that nothing ever
was done. It became apparent, however, even to distrustful
civil rights leaders that the official was no obstructionist. He
simply was operating in a maze of procedures. This perception
by civil rights leaders was important. It eased their suspicions
and helped create a more favorable bargaining climate.

Another characteristic, as noted above, is the very inade-
quate system of communications between the Superintendent and
the supervisory staff. There is not only a failure of communications downward, but also a lack of adequacy in reporting procedures and an absence of what might be called control mechanism
in the organization. As a result, on several occasions Dr. Gross
was completely unaware that obstructionist practices by his personnel violated pledges he had made to civil rights leaders. One
case involving a junior high school in the Bronx came to his attention through the UFT representative only as a result of teacher

---

[1]Sayre and Kaufman, op. cit., p. 282.

complaints. The point here is the need of further investigation of the structure to find out the reason for such lack of information at the top about activities at the lower levels.

Another pattern persisting throughout the integration issue is the lack of adequate communication to many interested groups both in the school system and the wider community about the substance of the Board's and the Superintendent's plans. It seems to have been quite common for the people in the school areas being considered for integration to learn about the plan only when it "leaked" from a supposedly closed meeting. Sometimes there would be no official word for a period of days or weeks after a rumor began to circulate. This silence only stirred up white parent anxieties, especially in Jackson Heights. As one informant commented somewhat cynically: "They are supposed to be educators, they are supposed to know so much about how to communicate, yet they are their own worst enemies when it comes to telling anybody what's going on." The Human Relations staff has only recently been strengthened with personnel to handle problems of communicating with supervisors, teachers, and parents on the scale demanded in the city. The lack of adequate preparation in any neighborhood for an integration plan is synonymous, as in the Jackson Heights situation, with the lack of responsible, moderate leadership in favor of the plan. Indeed, many groups, integrationist or not, have charged that little or no leadership has been shown at the local level by school officials.

Chapter 5

INDIRECT INFLUENCE: THE CONTEST
FOR POWER IN THE COMMUNITY

INTRODUCTION

The major source of integration controversy is the dissatisfaction of those with indirect influence in the wider community. These are the nongovernmental groups who attempt to persuade the wielders of direct influence, in this case the Board of Education and the Superintendent, what integration policy to adopt and implement. In order to be successful, these groups must have access to the formal channels of power, demonstrate their relevancy and wisdom, and display the strength and ability to exercise influence in the educational arena.

The main focus of the present study is to identify such city-wide groups and leaders, their policy positions, their alliances and ties with other groups, their internal structure, the publics or constituents which they represent and must be responsive to, and finally, their role in school integration politics. For example, some groups or leaders have mediating roles, like the Public Education Association whose executive director, Fred McLaughlin communicates with all groups, or David Livingston of the Conference on Quality Integrated Education, who has been so successful in quickly mobilizing a working consensus among civil rights and white liberal groups. Some play negotiating and bargaining roles, i.e., the civil rights leaders in their relationships and meetings with Dr. Gross. Still others take vetoing and negating roles like those of the local resistance groups.

Some of the major social forces in school integration controversies now can be mapped out. There appear to be four major constellations, although all are beset by internal schisms that persist even when they join forces on any particular point of view. Consensus is frequently short and unstable. Thus the term disorganized pluralism may be aptly applied to New York City politics generally and to its school integration politics in particular. Some astute observers of New York City politics

refer to the system as an overorganized pluralism in which interest groups are constantly pulling in different directions. Certainly the ethnic character of New York City politics, especially
on school integration issues, is manifest in visibly racial and
religious overtones.

The five constellations of satellites having indirect influence are: (1) the traditional educational groups known as the
establishment, with their long history of general concern for the
public schools; (2) the traditional intergroup relations organizations who have generally opposed and fought discriminatory practices in the community; (3) the Negro and Puerto Rican civil
rights organizations which now have turned some of their attention to integrating the schools but who also speak out on employment and housing; and (4) two bipolar neighborhood groups (PAT
and EQUAL) which are struggling to impede or facilitate
(respectively) integration plans at the local level.

THE ESTABLISHMENT

Three traditional educational groups influence most educational matters. They are known as the establishment. Theirs
is a stabilizing and mediating role in school integration matters.

The first is the Public Education Association, a coordinating body representing a number of very powerful constituents:
professional and business leader groups, some moderate religious leaders, and civic organizations. PEA has a fairly centralized structure with power invested in Fred McLaughlin, the
executive director, a system which enables it to act swiftly in
crisis situations.

Historically, despite the fact that it has had many conservative establishment groups as constituents, PEA has been very
influential in effecting school reforms. PEA is an excellent example of a civic group engaged in the politics of education. Sol
Cohen points to the paradox:

> The PEA likes to be thought above politics.
> Regardless of the impression it prefers to foster,
> the PEA has been throughout its career deeply in-
> volved in politics. Its chief raison d'etre has been
> to influence the decisions of . . . the Department
> of Education. In its efforts to influence decision-
> making in the New York City school system, the

> PEA has employed all the strategies and tactics
> available to a skilled and resourceful interest
> group in city politics. It has been remarkably suc-
> cessful in winning acceptance of its basic program. [1]

In 1955 PEA initiated school integration in New York City
with the publication of its study of the quality of ghetto schools.
This study was undertaken at the request of Arthur Levitt, then
Chairman of the Board. The finding revealed the unquestionably
inferior quality of education in Negro ghetto areas where there
were more substitute teachers, fewer with advanced degrees,
and inferior physical plants, books, library facilities, and so on.
On the basis of this study, which was the first to advance the
notion of de facto segregation, the Board set up special service
schools and extra resources in these areas. School districts
were rezoned to stimulate integration in areas pinpointed as
wastelands by the report.

PEA's official position is to endorse measures that will
help to achieve better racial balance and a higher quality of education for all, but with consideration of the price. The group
has opposed both Rev. Milton Galamison of the Harlem Parents'
Workshop and EQUAL as irresponsibly pursuing integration regardless of the cost. They also oppose the PAT groups. They
oppose mass busing of children and have defended vigorously the
neighborhood school concept. They oppose an indiscriminate use
of the Princeton Plan for New York City, although they supported
the four pairings instituted in September, 1964, mainly because
they felt that the Board had taken great pains to provide for
improvement in the quality of these paired schools. They proudly
noted that over $300,000 was spent on improving PS 92. Yet, so
concerned are they with maintaining white support of the public
schools that they feel that the Board could have foregone even
these four pairings, which they feel had the effect of mobilizing
the Board's integration plan. PEA is in communication with
moderate groups and is, in a sense, the great compromising
element in the city.

---

[1]Sol Cohen, <u>Progressives and Urban School Reform</u> (New York:
Bureau of Publications, Teachers College, Columbia University,
1964), pp. 226-227.

PEA perceives the importance of integration, but considers equally or more important such matters as reducing class size, improving teacher training, and establishing nursery schools for children in deprived areas. Integrationists view this insistence on quality education as a position calculated to avoid offending influential whites. Because of the images which McLaughlin and many civil rights leaders have of each other, as a result of positions each has taken over the years, there has been little communication between them in recent months. This silence is unfortunate, for McLaughlin (and the PEA) has many influential constituents and enjoys ready access to both Board and Superintendent, as well as the reliance of the Mayor upon him as a specialist in the educational arena.

The Citizens' Committee for Children is the second civic group concerned with education. This is a highly professionalized organization, concerned primarily with child development, and composed mainly of educators, social workers, child psychologists, psychiatrists. Like PEA, this small elite organization is capable of responding quickly to a situation, since there is no need for the consent of a variegated constituency. The Citizens' Committee, however, is much more militantly integrationist than PEA, having always maintained very close relations with civil rights leaders and the political world, especially with the liberal forces. Kenneth Clark, for example, is an active Board member. The Citizens' Committee also maintains close relations with HARYOU and Mobilization for Youth. Whatever close contacts the groups have had with moderate groups have been with The United Parents' Association (to be discussed later) rather than PEA. CCC leaders felt that PEA opposed mass busing in a manner that simply strengthened the conservative groups, rather than facilitating communication, understanding, and orderly change. The CCC view, one contrary to that of PEA and based on sophisticated psychological thinking, was that mass busing was no revolutionary concept, that schools have been busing children for a long time, and that the concern lest it hinder the children's development was irrational.

Although CCC enjoys the respect shown to many civil rights groups and white liberals, still it is moderate enough to acknowledge the political realities of their situation as Negroes--namely, that Negro leaders simply must deliver results or they will lose their following.

Mrs. Truda Lash, the Executive Director of the Citizens' Committee for Children, functions as a valuable link connecting the civil rights leaders and the more moderate groups. The Committee's leaders understand the problems of civil rights leaders much more clearly and show them greater tolerance than do other moderate civic groups. Several members of the Citizens' Committee board are very active in liberal and civil rights causes.

The third major citywide civic organization, the United Parents' Association, is quite different in nature from PEA and CCC. UPA has a mass membership of some 400,000 parents. Therefore, it is less free to act quickly in expressing a position on integration, representing as it does all the parent groups of the city school system. The great diversity of the city is reflected in the variety of parent groups, all in disagreement with each other on basic school policy. Also, UPA is the only one of the three traditional education groups that is neighborhood-based and thoroughly informed about local problems. In this regard it is interesting to note some slight correlation between the scope of an organizations' interest and operation and its integration outlook. The more neighborhood-based an organization is, the more its members favor the neighborhood school and oppose any major change for the sake of integration. This may account simply for some of the variation in group ideologies. Not all citywide organizations favor integration to the same degree, and, of course, factors other than organizational scope must be used to explain such differences. Yet the distinction between neighborhood and citywide scope and focus is important.

UPA's Executive Director, Harold Siegel, is one of the most knowledgeable of citywide leaders on the subject of school affairs. He is concerned about the threatened and real white exodus from the public schools. He fears that in the next decades New York City's schools will come to resemble those of Washington, D.C., where the whites are only a small minority, and that little can be done to stop this development. Rather than try to integrate schools that inevitably will become racially imbalanced, he urges the city to undertake a massive program to upgrade ghetto schools. His position is much like that of Dr. Kenneth Clark, a major spokesman for some in the Negro community. Siegel fears that the city may end up playing a numbers game that will fail completely to contribute to better quality of education.

Siegel adopts an iconoclastic position in most discussions with integrationist leaders. He takes the view that Negro and Puerto Rican children will inherit the public schools and there is simply no value in talking about racial balance. Furthermore, he claims that if the Negroes' aspirations for integrated schools are raised to unattainable levels, since there is every likelihood of a continued white exodus over the next decade, the Negroes' resentment ten years from now may lead to more serious uprisings than a couple of orderly boycotts. UPA, then, appears to be taking a long-range view which others refuse to do. The exigencies of the situation, however, with Negro ghettos in Harlem, Bedford-Stuyvesant, and Corona that are near the boiling point, make it difficult to urge long-range views upon integrationists who demand "Freedom Now."

UPA claims to be the only truly pro-integration group, working for the possible rather than the unattainable. The organization is on the firing line in all the subcommunities throughout the city as it attempts to draw the parents together so that integration may be attained. Three-quarters of the Negro and Puerto Rican Parents' Associations throughout the city belong to UPA. Frequently they work out their differences in the UPA headquarters in Manhattan and take back to their community an agreement that is binding. An area of greatest UPA activity has been in site selection, where frequently the organization has opposed the integrationist forces.

The main constituency of UPA, of course, comprises the Parents' Associations. UPA acts as a service organization to PA's around the city. It has always remained independent of various liberal groups and coalitions, such as the Intergroup Relations Committee of the 1950's or the recently formed Conference on Quality Integrated Education. One reason for such political independence is that the Association must mirror parent views. Therefore, UPA opposes mass busing. Siegel maintains that one cannot integrate New York City without busing 200,000 children fairly long distances. UPA also opposes Princeton Plan pairings as not at all conducive to integration in New York City unless they meet fairly stringent criteria which are concerned mainly with population trends in the area. UPA, with its local Parents' Associations, was instrumental in presenting evidence against the Board's original 30 pairings and reducing them to four. Civil rights and white liberal leaders have since come around to this position. Finally, UPA favors the neighborhood school concept, claiming that three generations of teachers and supervisors have been trained in this tradition and it would be asking too much of them suddenly to give it up. It is also asking too much of parents to send their children by subways and across crowded thoroughfares and to relate to schools that are miles away.

Again and again the UPA has pointed out that it is not only the racial composition that determines the quality of the school, it may be the teaching staff and principal as well. There are vast differences in achievement levels of children in different schools in Negro ghettos, yet nobody asks the reason. In keeping with his plea for a moderate pace, Siegel asks for more research for evidence in evaluating various integration plans. Such research would include the following kinds of questions: (1) What has happened to the open enrollment of children in New York City? Open enrollment has been in operation long enough to assess the impact of an integrated education experience on at least some ghetto children. (2) What is the IQ of nonwhite children in integrated West Side schools, compared to that of their counterparts in Negro ghetto schools? (3) Is the achievement of white middle class children less in integrated schools than in white segregated ones?

INTERGROUP RELATIONS ORGANIZATIONS

New York City has a number of traditional intergroup organizations. They have long been interested in abating the practice of discrimination. They have also attempted to reduce the group hostilities based on the ethnic differences between nationality, religion, and race. These intergroup organizations include the American Jewish Committee, the American Jewish Congress, the Anti-Defamation League, the Catholic Interracial Council, the Protestant Council of Churches, and the Civil Liberties Union. Some have actively supported measures to integrate the public schools. Some were members of the Intergroup Committee organized in the 1950's and presently support the Conference for Quality Integrated Education. The old Intergroup Committee became ineffective even before the 1964 boycotts. The Committee was unable to hold together any kind of working consensus and was torn apart by what seemed to be almost permanent divisions. The alliance between the Jewish liberal groups and Negro civil rights groups became increasingly difficult to maintain, partly because of the hostility toward the white liberal in the militant Negro group, partly because of the many negative encounters with some segments of the Jewish community. The images that various ethnic groups have of one another must be explored, for they are one key to understanding the sources for and the nature of political alliances and schisms.

A key white liberal organization that has taken a strong integrationist stance is the Conference for Quality Integrated Education. The Conference was formed shortly after the first Negro boycott and assumed a major role in policy-making sessions with Dr. Gross. The purpose of the Conference was to mend fences in the white liberal community and expand what its leaders constantly refer to as the dialogue between white liberals and civil rights organizations. It has been ably led by David Livingston, a skillful labor negotiator who has been active in civil rights causes since the 1940's, and Rev. Donald Harrington of the Community Church of New York, a respected leader of the social action Protestant community. The first meeting was attended by several hundred people, mostly white, and included many politicians--state legislators and city councilmen--and some Negro leaders. This was one of the largest turnouts of a white liberal group for a civil rights cause.

The first meeting was devoted to a series of statements by various white liberal leaders who had felt completely alone on the school integration issue. Many said that in trying to do the right thing and coming out forthrightly in favor of integration plans, they had been all but ostracized by their members and constituents. The term white backlash, first used in this meeting to describe New York City politics, was later to appear in national political discussions.

The organizations participating in this meeting (most of whom still are members) included most of the civic and political groups in New York City that had traditionally been identified with liberal causes, with the exception of some unions. Among them were the American Jewish Committee, the American Jewish Congress, the Anti-Defamation League, the National Council of Jewish Women, Union Theological Seminary, the Civil Liberties Union, the Catholic Interracial Council, the Lutheran Human Relations Association of Greater New York, the Liberal Party, Americans for Democratic Action, the Protestant Council, the Jewish Labor Committee, the Ethical Culture Society, the

Puerto Rican Forum, the Office of the Commonwealth of Puerto Rico, and others. Politicians included State Senator Manfred Ohrenstein, City Councilmen Theodore Weiss and Paul O'Dwyer, and U.S. Congressman William F. Ryan. Finally, the civil rights groups were well represented by leaders from the NAACP, the Urban League of New York, CORE, SNICC, the Harlem Parents' Committee, and the Intergroup Committee on New York City Schools.

It is clear from the preceding list that the Conference included groups of varied positions. Until the time when PAT threatened to boycott the schools, all these moderates were satisfied to be represented in the Conference by Livingston and Harrington. Since Livingston made a sharp statement to the press referring to PAT as bigoted and racist, however, the Jewish groups have had a more tenuous commitment to the Conference.

After May, 1964, the Conference played a major role in the formulation and modification of Dr. Gross's integration program. As one long-time civil rights leader put it: "The Conference became the vehicle through which the white liberal community caught up with its own visions and equivocations." An early public statement from the Conference expressed its strong support of the Allen Report and put the white liberal community on record as favoring what they considered a plan for basic structural changes in the school system. The Conference then rejected the Gross plan which followed shortly thereafter. While the Conference generally mended fences in the white liberal community and created an operable consensus, it also reached out to Negro organizations. A working coalition was formed when all liberal and civil rights leaders received telegrams from Dr. Gross the day after he released his plans, asking them to meet with him to discuss his program. A successful first meeting led to several later ones, which now are held on a regular basis.

THE NEGRO AND PUERTO RICAN CIVIL RIGHTS ORGANIZATIONS

Much has been written about deep-rooted splits in the Negro civil rights movement. There certainly are schisms in New York City among those leaders concerned with hastening integration efforts. Although the civil rights partisans feel that newspapers have distorted the situation, it is true that there are major splits in the civil rights camp on school integration issues. There was a temporary consensus in June, 1963, when Roy Wilkins rallied civil rights groups into a coordinating committee to press for implementation by school boards of Commissioner Allen's order to move toward racial balance in schools. Rev. Milton Galamison was appointed chairman of that committee, with the responsibility for merging and representing the views of the members: CORE, the Urban League, NAACP, Harlem Parents, and his own groups. During the summer, however, he spoke independently, often in opposition to the views of all except the most militant. This resulted in the withdrawal of NAACP, the Urban League, and CORE.

Moderate consensus developed again when Dr. Gross and the Board delayed formulation of an integration program, particularly after a proposed September boycott was called off to await the proposal promised by the first of December. This consensus was wide and held firm through the February boycott. Only Galamison and his groups openly promoted the second boycott, while the national offices of CORE and NAACP as well as the Urban League were very much opposed. Roy Wilkins declared, "We should let the children go to school while the adults argue," a statement which represented the sentiments of James Farmer and most other civil rights and white liberal leaders.

The divisions continued throughout the summer of 1964, while civil rights leaders began to meet regularly in closed sessions with Dr. Gross to discuss his various plans to facilitate school integration in the coming years. Certainly the internal differences among civil rights groups reduced their bargaining effectiveness, for they represented unresolved differences of opinion.

Galamison and some others represent an earlier style of Negro leadership, the charismatic rallying element who can sweep a movement on to make broad demands for rapid and drastic change without going into great detail about the method. Wilkins and even Farmer are more pragmatic. They realize that more is to be gained by developing specific programs and bargaining with the white power structure rather than staging repeated mass demonstrations and boycotts that might backfire in an election year. A third type is Bayard Rustin, who remains apart from any groups, convinced that most of the discussion about school integration is trivial, that even the civil rights

movement in general is insignificant because of its basically conservative nature, and that the movement should take on a more
revolutionary tone. [1]

The differences between and among the Negro civil rights
groups representing the minorities--Negro and Puerto Rican--
are due in part to their various organizational structures, memberships, leadership goals, strategies, and tactics. CORE has
a dozen chapters, all quite autonomous and independent of each
other and of the national office, which is in New York. Each
chapter has the authority to plan its own projects. About the
only constitutional provision which might be construed as a lim-
itation is that the programs must be nonviolent and that the chapters develop reasonable goals and tactics by which to achieve
them. Generally this means that the major purpose of CORE is
not to threaten but to negotiate, to point up inequities in terms of
the physical conditions under which certain minority groups live.

The power of any CORE chapter is based not on the size of
its membership but on how well it explains issues to the citizens
in its surrounding blocks. The calculation is as follows: a very
good chapter has between 25 and 50 street-carrying members,
which means that they will engage in very active campaigning
when called upon, for instance, in a boycott. These people will
contact between 2,000 and 5,000 and maybe even 10,000 people
in churches, in projects, and other community gatherings.

The chapters are divided into two basic groups. Some
prefer a democratic involvement of their members in decision-
making, while the leaders of other chapters demand more direct
action toward integration. These latter groups have very little
contact with their communities. They are more interested in
forming coalitions and developing strategies and tactics than in
dealing with the substantive educational issues.

The NAACP is a large mass organization with its national
office as well as a dozen branches in New York City. Its explicit
policy in support of school integration provides the basis for consensus among the branches. The city leaders depend on the local
branches for policy guidance. The militant nature of the locals

---

[1] Nat Hentoff, interview with Bayard Rustin, The Village
Voice (New York), August 30, 1964.

leaves little freedom to city leaders. Thus, NAACP has participated actively in demonstrations and in the February boycott. At the same time, however, they continue to negotiate with administrators and pursue legal remedies in the courts. NAACP's interest in the school integration controversy began in 1957 and the organization now plays a central role in developing Negro strategy.

NAACP has pursued a fairly consistent policy on school integration matters. It became involved almost accidentally when its Legal Defense Fund played a very active role in the Malverne case on Long Island. The NAACP complaint of imbalance in the Malverne schools occasioned Commissioner Allen's directive to school boards throughout the state to send him their plans for creating racial balance where it did not presently exist.

The NAACP position, on which there was considerable consensus among the local branches following Roy Wilkins' reaction to Commissioner Allen's directive, generally favored rapid measures to increase integration. They supported the Board's original idea of 30 or more pairings. Later they endorsed the Allen Report, as did all other civil rights groups. Over the spring and summer their position changed as they became increasingly aware of the limited function of pairings in New York City. Their support of pairings decreased as they approached the moderates' view that pairings were helpful for integration only under very specific and atypical circumstances.

On many occasions Roy Wilkins has taken a somewhat more moderate position than the local branches, although this apparently has not caused repercussions in the organization. Wilkins opposes boycotts per se, regardless of their purpose, and he also opposes mass busing. His views on the latter issue are based less on his commitment to voluntarism than on his fear of the resentment it might evoke in the white community and the possibility that it could lead to an increasing white exodus from Manhattan or at least from the public school system.

While NAACP has been able to reach a consensus on its school integration position and react effectively to many situations, this has not been the case for CORE. The lack of agreement may be due to a difference in internal structure and politics. CORE was more recently formed and on a much more decentralized and federated basis than was NAACP. As a result CORE has had no single policy. Moreover, it has tended to attract more militant, activist members than NAACP, which is considered conservative by a younger generation of militants. CORE is less effective, since it has no unified position or spokesman. The Brooklyn and Bronx chapters of CORE are the most militant and the other branches tend to follow their lead. Unlike the NAACP, CORE has tended to rush into critical situations after they have developed.

The Urban League, on the other hand, played a key role from 1954 to 1957. This group took early cognizance of the school integration problem and now plays an advisory role. It is an elite organization with powerful members from both the white and Negro communities. While in general the League does not support boycotts, it did approve the action of February, 1964. There is little or no mass membership to represent and thus the leaders can move freely. They have traditionally been concerned about providing opportunities for the urban Negroes. They have concentrated on job opportunities and perceive education as directly related.

In the summer of 1963, following Commissioner Allen's order, these three Negro civil rights organizations joined with the Harlem Parents' Committee and the Parents' Workshop for Equality to form the Citywide Committee for Integrated Schools and coordinate their efforts. Rev. Galamison was designated-- not elected--as chairman to represent the Committee on various occasions in negotiating or bargaining. Gradually, however, this ceased to be a coordinating group which represented the views or consensus of the five previously mentioned. It took on a separate identity. In the process Galamison, as chairman, decided and announced various actions which were not at all in line with the goals and stated positions of the constituent members. Unable to return the Committee to its former status, thereby coordinating the efforts of these five groups and achieving some kind of consensus, NAACP withdrew. Later CORE withdrew and the Urban League only half remained, restating its right to participate in the Citywide Committee when it chose. The Citywide Committee for Integrated Schools remains in formal existence but in effect it has no constituency. It has become Galamison's organization.

Nevertheless, Negro leaders in New York City have reached agreement on some general fundamentals. They have unanimously

endorsed the Allen Report which seemed to them, even to
Galamison, a revolutionary document despite its complete acceptance of the neighborhood school for the first four grades.
In fact, the Allen report rallied them together once more as they
began a summer of meetings with Dr. Gross. Group cohesion
within the Negro leadership seems to be greatest when promises
of change and substantial concession by white leaders seem too
good to lose by bickering among themselves over details. On the
other hand, whenever integration plans fail to meet the schedule,
some civil rights faction threatens to bolt the meetings and stage
its own boycott or demonstration. Rev. Galamison led this dis-
sident faction, stating on many occasions that his followers were
"tired of words, studies, and broken promises." Willingness to
stay with the situation and continue bargaining, much more characteristic of the new style of Negro leader, is not at all unanimous.

Over the past several months there has been much discussion over whether or not Negro leaders like Galamison really
represent a majority of rank-and-file Negro parents. Although
the answer is politically important, there are no adequate data
available for more than speculation. One study suggested that
as many as half the Negroes interviewed opposed mass busing.[1]
This is no longer an issue of any importance, however, because
the Allen Report proposed many structural changes in the system
that do not require busing. In fact, the report strongly suggested
that mass busing, like pairings, is not the answer. At this stage
the Negro leaders are well in advance of their followers in their
consent to bus children out of local neighborhoods, for many
Negroes are just as intent on preserving the status quo as some
conservative whites. A case can be made for this attempt to
lead Negro parents on the issue against their presently stated
wishes. After an historical experience that included both slavery
and second-class citizenship, many American Negroes have
seriously limited their aspirations, for fear of once more being
put down by the white community, as Charles Silberman[2] has
pointed out so well. Acceptance of the Negroes' present level of
aspiration as a guide to public policy will not further the cause
of equal opportunity.

---

[1] The New York Times, July 27, 1964.

[2] Charles E. Silberman, Crisis in Black and White (New York:
Random House, 1964).

Finally, the Puerto Rican community participates through two agencies, the Commonwealth of Puerto Rico and the Puerto Rican Forum. Neither group has become too involved with the Negro civil rights movement, yet both supported the February boycott. However, they organized their own demonstration before City Hall on a Sunday in March, 1964. The other civil rights organizations are considerably perturbed by the failure of the Puerto Ricans to exert their influence in formulating integration policy.

The Puerto Ricans have made few demands on school officials except to provide special educational services for their children whose language handicaps make it difficult for them to adjust to English-speaking classrooms. Also, the Puerto Rican community questions the validity of counting their children in with Negro children when calculating the racial distribution.

BIPOLAR NEIGHBORHOOD: TWO ORGANIZATIONS

The final constellation consists of two newly formed antagonistic organizations with their roots in the local neighborhood but represented by articulate citywide spokesmen. Both have the single purpose of taking a stand on school integration and mobilizing parent support. Interestingly enough, both are led by women. Mrs. Rosemary Gunning is the executive secretary of the anti-integration Parents and Taxpayers Coordinating Council (PAT), and Mrs. Ellen Lurie is the spokesman for EQUAL, composed of representatives of groups dedicated to quality integrated education.

Mrs. Gunning represents the Joint Council of Parents and Taxpayers groups, the first of which was formed in September, 1963, in Queens. Its purpose was to fight the announced pairing and other integration plans. A similar organization formed in January, 1964, in Brooklyn is known as the Joint Council for Better Education. Both are grassroots organizations, in contrast to most other citywide groups, and both strongly oppose virtually all the integration plans that have been formulated by Dr. Gross and the Board of Education since Commissioner Allen's order of May, 1963. Both are loosely knit federations, representing a variety of interests throughout the city, though concentrated more heavily in Queens, Brooklyn, and the Bronx in that order. They are almost exclusively white and are bound together by their opposition to any plan that calls for the involuntary transfer of children from the neighborhood schools.

PAT officials claim to represent some hundred organizations and a total of more than 200,000 persons. The Joint Council says it represents 750,000 persons in its 61 affiliated groups. Among these are three Brooklyn Parents and Taxpayers groups. Each organization sends three delegates to the Joint Council's steering committee. The two organizations have worked together in various political protests against the Board's integration plans and have served as a united front to preserve the neighborhood schools concept.

Mrs. Ellen Lurie represents EQUAL, the one group within the civil rights-white liberal coalition that is in close touch with the neighborhoods. The organization was formed as an outgrowth of discussions held in March, 1964, by individuals from all over the city. They were called together on the initiative of Mr. Harry Ansorge, former chairman of the Jackson Heights Committee for Balanced Schools. This committee was formerly called the Metropolitan Council for Integrated Quality Schools and was organized with the avowed purpose of helping parents living in predominantly white communities to exert as much influence as possible in the fight to secure quality integrated education. It is primarily a grassroots organization working in Brooklyn, the Bronx, Manhattan, and Queens. In Brooklyn a Committee to Advance Racial Integration in the Schools (CARIS) was formed in mid-February, 1964, drawing its membership from Brooklyn Heights, Sheepshead Bay, Flatbush, East Flatbush, Coney Island, Canarsie, Bensonhurst, Crown Heights, Kensington, and East New York. In addition, there is a group in Sheepshead Bay which calls itself Parents for Integrated Quality Pilot Schools and claims a membership of about seventy-five white families who would like to bus their children into a school in Bedford-Stuyvesant. A Brownsville-East New York-Canarsie-East Flatbush group formed a committee to develop positive community attitudes toward integration and study the feasibility of educational parks in a nearby urban renewal area. In Brooklyn Heights a Community Schools Committee was established by parents in PS 7 (mainly Negro) and PS 8 (mainly white) to work together for pairing of the two schools. Both Parents' Associations voted support and the white parents asked that busing be included because of the traffic at street crossings.

There is a Bronx Committee for Integrated Schools, affiliated with the Bronx Civil Rights Action Committee, which draws on leaders from the East Bronx, Mid-Bronx, Riverdale, Kingsbridge, Pelham Parkway, and Marblehill. They worked to prevent some pairings suggested by the Board which seemed to promise little in terms of either integration or quality education. A group called MARK (Marblehill-Riverdale-Kingsbridge) has a committee working for civil rights in the fields of housing and employment as well as education. MARK was an outgrowth of the March on Washington in August, 1963. There is also a Riverdale Committee on Intergroup Relations.

Manhattan has groups in Inwood (the Upper Manhattan Civil Rights Committee, the Inwood Schools Committee and a Washington Heights and Inwood Committee for Integrated Quality Education) which sponsor lectures and conferences where the community can thrash out the educational advantages of integration plans. The Riverside-Edgecombe (NENA) group in a transitional area along Riverside Drive works to improve local schools so that more white residents will send their children there. A group in Morningside Heights is pushing for improvement of the local public schools so that more residents will use them. A West Side branch of EQUAL which deals with achieving more integrated quality education inside the schools already has been active in the Lincoln Square area. There are groups in Yorkville, Chelsea, the Lower East Side, and Greenwich Village.

EQUAL, then, is actively attempting to do what many civil rights leaders feel the Board of Education has been unable to do--communicate with parents in an attempt to deflate anxieties and panic, explain the virtues of integrated education, induce local opinion leaders such as the clergy to play an active role in supporting integration, and introduce a number of specific programs like interschool visits, open house before the opening of school, school meetings of the clergy with parents at key times such as opening day. However, EQUAL has a very mixed image with some moderate groups who criticize it as an irresponsible and destructive force.

The following excerpt from a television debate between the leaders of the two groups on the eve of the September, 1964, boycott illustrates the divergence of opinion.

Mrs. Gunning. Well, we have an excellent voluntary plan. Parents who are not satisfied with the
integration set-up in the schools which their children
attend are permitted to transfer to a school that has a
larger group of children of another race. This perhaps
should be enlarged somewhat, but we feel that it should
be tackled from a voluntary standpoint when children
are leaving their immediate neighborhoods.

Moderator. If I read you correctly, you admit
that there is a problem of racial imbalance in the city
schools, but that the solution of that problem should be
left in the hands of the individual parents, not in the
hands of the Board of Education through compulsory
transfer.

Mrs. Gunning. Yes, I think there are some
things the Board can do in the zoning and things of that
type where they are not compulsorily transferring children from their own neighborhoods.

Moderator. Well, Mrs. Gunning, I think it
might help if we have a definition of neighborhood. The
reason I ask is that some of the schools that are being
paired are only a short distance apart, even though
they do have different ethnic compositions.

Mrs. Gunning. Well, those schools were zoned
that way for specific school administrative reasons,
and that is because there were hazardous crossings.
This Board has overlooked this fact in the pairings,
and the result is that they are subordinating what we
feel is the safety of the children by sending them across
these hazardous crossings.

Moderator. Well, what is the neighborhood
school? Is it a school that is nearest to you or is it
a school in your community that may be a few blocks
from another school.

Mrs. Gunning. Well, the way the schools are
set up, they are sometimes close together, but you
will find that is because they serve different neighborhoods. The reason that the neighborhoods are considered the zoning criteria for those schools is because

of the topographical situation that confronted the Board. This is sound school administration all over the country.

Moderator. Mrs. Gunning, Mrs. Lurie has a comment on that, if we may.

Mrs. Lurie. I think that we have to separate the fantasy from the facts. All over the country we have consolidated school districts where people go to a central school district from many parts of the county. The rural areas are used to having very large neighborhoods in which to go to school. We used to have neighborhood schools that went through the eighth grade. Then we decided that educationally it was desirable to move the adolescents into a different kind of setup, the junior high school, and so the neighborhood up to the sixth grade--the attendance district--became one thing, the attendance district for the seventh, eighth, and ninth grades became quite another thing. Mrs. Gunning is right, of course, to say that they vary in density. Therefore in Queens there may be a neighborhood for a school out near Francis Willard Boulevard where everybody has to go by bus. I know that up in Inwood where I live, where PS 98 is located, almost all the children either have to charter their own bus or go with the school bus to get to their neighborhood schools. The neighborhood has become a myth. We are constantly changing the idea of neighborhood. The idea of the neighborhood was to choose attendance districts where everybody in the city could get equal educational opportunity. If the neighborhoods ghettoize themselves or segregate themselves, and we decide that integrated education is very important, then we do not retain the present tactic for forcing neighborhood schools, but rather we take the goal of equal opportunity for all children and choose a different tactic, a different kind of attendance area.

Mrs. Gunning. If I may reply to Mrs. Lurie briefly, we must remember that in consolidated schools and in the selection of an urban area, the parents made the decision as to where they wish their children to go to school. In older New York City, the parents selected

the schools and moved near them. Now they do not
have a voice in this removal. They do not have an
elected board, as in most sections of the country.

Moderator. Mr. Mahalek, now it's your turn.

Mr. Mahalek. Mrs. Gunning, your organization
promised in March of this year to stage the largest
protest demonstration in the history of City Hall. And
by most accounts you did just that, about 15,000 people
turned out. Do you think this boycott proposed for
September will be the largest boycott of its kind, and
if so, how big?

Mrs. Gunning. Well, that is hard to say. We
have no idea how many people will respond to this.
We have every evidence that it will be large. In exact
numbers, it's hard to predict. I couldn't have predicted, I thought about 5,000 people would turn out on
March 12, and in spite of the estimate of 15,000, most
people think 25,000 turned out. Now whether that will
be repeated tomorrow with the school, we will have
to wait and see.

Mr. Mahalek. You won't estimate how many
children will stay home, but what would you call a
successful figure, how many would have to stay out
for you to say that your demonstration was in fact a
success?

Mrs. Gunning. We are not considering figures,
but we are trying to impress upon the Board of Education that the children who are absent tomorrow should
not be included in a plan for involuntary removal, because they will not comply.

Mr. Mahalek. Well, what could they do about
it? How could they not go?

Mrs. Gunning. We are going to proceed with
our present plans. First we are going to intensify our
efforts to get proper legislative response to the parents' wishes, and we will of course continue in the
courts, because we have not yet had our final voice.

Mr. Mahalek. But that will take many, many months, certainly four or five months. What will happen to the youngsters in the meantime? I know that you have plans for some private schools of your own, at least two that I have heard about.

Mrs. Gunning. There will be. Every one of the children who remain out indefinitely, that is the children who have been involuntarily transferred, will be provided adequate education all the time that they are out of school.

Mrs. Lurie. As you mentioned earlier, EQUAL is planning action to point up some of the things that PAT is doing. Mrs. Gunning just mentioned the private school that they are setting up, and it might be appropriate to discuss this right now. This afternoon, right after I leave this program as a matter of fact, I will be going out to Jackson Heights. At 4:00 this afternoon we are going to start a twenty-four-hour vigil of reconciliation, Mrs. Gunning, not of recrimination, for EQUAL is not going to call PAT any names at all, we are not going to shout or hold picket signs up. But we will be coming very quietly--clergy, parents, and teachers from all over the city, from all the boroughs--to watch in shifts of two hours at a time. Six of us at a time will bear witness to the fact that this boycott is immoral, that this is in fact turning our backs on our public schools. We have got to face our common problems together. There has to be adequate education, as you said so well before, it is something that all of us want for our children. Finding the right way to have it is a very hard job in the city schools, but we will be saying during this vigil which will start at 4:00 today and go on until 4:00 tomorrow, right outside the private school that PAT is renting in the basement of one of the apartment houses in Jackson Heights, Don't withdraw and turn your backs. Let's not say one brother fights the other. Let's try to find something that we all admit is of the highest possible value--integrated education.

Moderator. Have you any plans for any other direct action or demonstrations?

Mrs. Lurie. This is not going to be solved by
shouting and demonstrations. The emotion in the
streets right now is something fierce. For example,
the amount of misinformation that people have, the
amount of fear that people have that there are not going to be the same groupings anymore, they are not
going to have SP or special progress classes. Earlier
today the PAT people accused a school out in Queens
of vandalism and said that the children there were so
dangerous that the Board of Education had to use
wooden forks and spoons instead of silver. When I
left the program I was shocked at this and immediately called up Eastern Queens and found that this is
not true, that silverware just got lost and they ordered
plastic utensils. But what they pointed out is that all
junior high schools in our city admittedly have a problem with adolescents. I would like to point out to
PAT and Mrs. Gunning that we have a problem of
adolescents because we are practicing one thing and
preaching another. We say that in America, in a
democracy, we have wonderful high values of justice
and equal opportunity and brotherhood, and then as
parents we turn around and act quite the opposite.
All psychiatrists--famous pediatricians like Dr.
Spock--will say that this is harming our children,
that they turn out disrespectful of the law, disrespectful of the church, disrespectful of adults, because we don't practice what we preach. This is far
more detrimental than walking a few more blocks to
school.

Chapter 6

TWO STRATEGIES FOR POWER

Most of the dramatis personae who are identified above engage in constant efforts to prevail over integration policy. The behavioral patterns reported here provide the raw materials of the politics of education. The first section describes how the pro-integration forces developed a dialogue with the Superintendent and their efforts to bargain and negotiate for liberal policy as well as for better implementation of plans already adopted. The section illustrates the efforts of conservatives who, feeling powerless to secure any modification of integration plans, developed the strategy of securing citizen support for their position in the form of a mass movement at the local school level.

A LEADERSHIP DIALOGUE

A dialogue between then Superintendent Calvin Gross and the pro-integration forces was established following the announcement of the 1964-1965 plans. The meetings were a form of bargaining or negotiating. There were no written agreements and no mechanisms to adjudicate in cases of alleged breach of faith or good will. Yet Dr. Gross seriously considered the views and imaginative ideas of liberal leaders and modified many parts of his plan in the course of meeting with them, suggesting that the analogy to collective bargaining sessions was not without empirical justification. At the outset Dr. Gross established ground rules according to which the meetings would range over a number of specific issues. Through mutual exploration of these specific issues he and the liberal leaders would formulate general policy, and in fact they would proceed as if there were no existing Board or school policy.

These meetings, at least the early sessions, facilitated a closing of ranks and effected a working consensus within the white liberal-civil rights camp for the first time in the history of school integration controversies in New York City. Many participants observed that the meetings were revolutionary departures from past Board and Superintendent practice. Issue that never before had been subject to negotiation were discussed rationally between Dr. Gross and a widely representative liberal group that was united for the first time. Unfortunately for the liberal group, its consensus, so effectively engineered by David Livingston, was short-lived and some groups constantly threatened to withdraw or at least disagreed strongly with the majority point of view.

Livingston and Harrington were skillful negotiators, sophisticated in analyzing the social forces that had to be mobilized to assure success. From the start they tried to enlarge their constituency to include the more moderate groups. They contacted Fred McLaughlin of the Public Education Association and attempted to enlist the support of Harold Siegel of the United Parents Association and the Citizens' Committee for Children. A five-hour meeting that took place in late spring included Livingston, Harrington, McLaughlin, and Harold Shiff of the ADL, but to no avail. The PEA has many ties with such moderate conservative groups as the City Club, the state bar association, influential business and labor leaders, the Mayor, the Democratic party, and others. PEA has been progressive in its activities for school integration over the years. They sponsored one of the first studies in 1955 on the quality of schools in ghetto areas and coined the term de facto segregation. However, PEA could not endorse a conference that included organizations too militant for its own views. Nor did the UPA join the Conference. They were even more restricted by constituent groups that were neighborhood-based and more conservative than PEA on the subject of integration.

A brief chronology of the meetings between Dr. Gross and the civil rights groups during that summer will suggest the range of issues on which the latter were attempting to exert their influence. At the first meeting in June the liberal leaders told Dr. Gross of their regret (1) that he had so watered down the Allen plan in his own report to the Board and (2) that the first frank discussion between him and liberal spokesmen about plans for the fall occurred only after he had released them to the press. Apparently this was to avoid his seeming the captive of any group. Despite these disagreements, four six-hour meetings took place in early June. Information about these meetings was withheld from the press in order to create a climate that would encourage free exchange.

Dr. Gross's initial position, from which he retreated in the course of the first few meetings, was that he had Hobson's choice between improving radically the quality of education in the Negro ghetto and moving immediately to take Negro children from their neighborhood by means of pairing and mass transportation. One upshot of the meetings was that Gross was encouraged to re-define the situation so that both goals (moving children around and upgrading the ghetto schools) would be worthwhile.

A few very specific issues, all related to the Allen Report, were the focus of discussion throughout the summer. The first question was how to handle the many sixth grade children who were moving from segregated Harlem schools into junior highs. The civil rights groups suggested that sixth graders from ghetto schools be distributed to underutilized, white junior high schools. This would help rid the system of the substantial amount of seg-regation at the junior high level. Dr. Gross considered this a good idea, but it took several days to gain acceptance. Finally, he agreed on a compromise plan which, while it may have aliena-ted some of the militant integrationists, did not break up the meeting. He agreed to offer parents of sixth grade children a choice of transferring to underutilized white junior high schools or remaining in segregated ones. There was much discussion about the method, which finally was established on a permissive rather than a consignment basis.

A second issue, more general in nature, bore on the rela-tion between Dr. Gross's plan and the Allen Report. Gross said that he accepted the Allen Report in its entirety, although with some reservations because of its extremely general nature. He claimed that his plan was consciously formulated as a first step to implement the Allen Report, whose provisions he felt could be put into effect only over a long time period. Civil rights leaders pointed out that the press version had led most interested parties to conclude that his plan was either in direct opposition to Allen's or at the very least represented a serious dilution. In fact, some white liberal groups had opposed the Allen Report and em-braced that of Gross, who stated emphatically that the Allen Re-port was the single most effective measure in getting the Board to take action. This implied criticism of the Board may have facilitated the negotiations, for it became apparent to some that Gross was now exerting stronger leadership.

81

The one serious reservation held by Gross about the Allen Report was the 4-4-4 plan, the basis for the whole structural reorganization. There is little empirical evidence that this plan is better educationally than others. Clearly the 4-4-4 plan would improve the educational quality in ghetto areas without hurting it elsewhere. The principal result would be to empty two grades from grammar schools so that nursery school classes of ages 3-5 could be started on a saturation basis. The burden of proof rests not with the proponents of the plan but with the skeptics.

It seemed to civil rights leaders that Dr. Gross had changed his conceptions of his role since first coming to the city. Apparently while he was still learning his new position he defined the role in somewhat narrow, technical terms, as do many educational administrators. He proceeded in the usual manner of educators to consider that school and political matters must be kept separate. The two boycotts seemed to change this opinion, and as the spring wore on and he was pressed by civil rights leaders, PAT, factions within his own board, and his school supervisors, he began to consider his situation in political terms. He saw that his position in the city was insecure and that in the long run the civil rights groups might become his staunchest allies. Since he had been estranged from the Board, he needed supporters desperately and welcomed opportunities to build up a relationship with what he believed to be a responsible segment of the community who shared many of his views, despite some militant members.

Within the civil rights-white liberal camp consensus was unstable. Some members suspected Dr. Gross's intentions or doubted his ability to keep promises. Others, however, were interested in continuing to meet and negotiate. The degree of consensus ranged from a fairly general agreement on long-range goals and a willingness to work together at the early stages (June and July) to periodic threats of withdrawal on the part of some groups (Parents' Workshop, Harlem Parents, and CORE) when it became evident that Gross's own supervisory staff was not implementing his integration plans. About September 10, a few days before school was to open, there seemed to be broad public consensus on the minimum program put forth by Dr. Gross. There were rumblings of discontent, for example, one civil rights leader's initial unwillingness to sign a statement endorsing Dr. Gross's plan. However, when PAT announced its boycott intentions, cohesion once more prevailed in the liberal camp. Each time the opposition dramatized its case, civil rights and moderate groups became reconciled.

When the meetings with Dr. Gross began, there were a number of points of agreement among the negotiators. All favored the Allen Report and opposed Gross's proposals. All were in favor of continuing discussions with him to see how far they could carry the dialogue. They were pleased with the extent to which they saw his position change as a result of their meetings. Furthermore, many Board policies which most civil rights leaders had originally interpreted as conscious acts against integration turned out on closer examination to be simple bureaucratic oversight. One civil rights leader remarked that he had never seen a bureaucracy quite so riddled with compulsive rule followers who were so enmeshed in procedure that they had lost all perspective of the outside world.

As the meetings proceeded during the summer a number of agreements were hammered out on specific matters. (1) Dr. Gross promised that the city would not build any new schools in segregated areas, especially in Negro ghettos. (2) By 1965 the segregated junior high schools would be eliminated and a good beginning would be made in building middle schools on an integrated basis, as part of Commissioner Allen's educational parks concept. Dr. Gross promised that some of these middle schools would be started in 1965. (3) He promised always to discuss from their very inception any plans for integration with civil rights groups rather than calling them in after decisions and plans had been made simply to inform them of faits accomplis.

Yet there were also areas of strong disagreement between Dr. Gross and these groups. Civil rights leaders were especially upset about the permissive character of the assignment plan for sixth graders to move into underutilized white junior high schools. The more militant wing was extremely displeased, having become disenchanted with open enrollment over the years. Open enrollment frequently has been used as a defensive maneuver by white leaders to dampen integration efforts. In Manhattan, however, up to 50 per cent of the Negro parents given this option chose it, although in other areas the percentage was much lower.

At one point in late June or early July, after the negotiations had proceeded quite far, civil rights groups learned that some supervisory personnel--associate and assistant superintendents and principals--were not following Dr. Gross's recommendations at all. In fact, they were persuading parents in Negro areas not to send their children from their neighborhood schools into some new white areas in the Bronx where they had never been before. In a sense, these people were vetoing plans and policies that had already been agreed on at the bargaining table. This conflict was taken up with Dr. Gross at the next meeting. It became clear that the supervisors were reinterpreting Gross's general policy directives to fit their own needs and interests. Two techniques were particularly noticeable: (1) teachers and principals encouraged the Negro parents to maintain the status quo, and (2) high-level supervisors would impose procedures upon teachers that lowered their morale and willingness to accept change.

One critical incident has much broader implications for understanding how the educational bureaucracy has thwarted integration efforts. In one junior high in the Bronx, where the Allen concept of middle schools was being put into effect, ninth graders were being moved into high schools and sixth graders into the junior high or emerging middle schools. The vacancies in the grammar schools created by the exodus of the sixth and later the fifth graders were filled with nursery school children from depressed areas who were to be served on a saturation plan basis. Apparently there was such resentment among teachers in one school that a UFT local representative protested to the central UFT headquarters about the teaching conditions. Principals were imposing burdens on teachers in the school that could well have been avoided: (1) The same teachers were being compelled to teach both English and social studies classes, despite city and state rules that prevent such activity, commonly designated as teaching out of license. Both subjects were placed in the same block of class time. (2) Though the UFT had bargained for a yearly decrease of one class period a week, one high level superior is reported to have told teachers, "You can't have two experiments at the same time, so you won't get any reduction of one period this year." (3) Since the need for shop teachers inevitably decreased with the exodus of ninth graders, and the new sixth grade was judged not quite ready, some teachers had to look for new situations. Several were kept waiting for a week or more instead of being helped to relocate. (4) Many new clerical burdens were imposed on the teachers. Since the number of graduating and entering classes was doubled (ninth and eighth graders would exit while sixth and seventh would enter), the volume of various health records, reading, IQ, and other scores increased. The upshot was that teachers picketed the school and were supported by some parents.

There are some explanations for this resistance to the middle school plans. First, supervisors and teachers generally have resisted major reorganization. Second, junior high school principals long had been lobbying to have their salaries made equivalent to those of high school principals, arguing that they had equal responsibilities and training.

Now that the middle schools would include fifth and sixth grades, these demands were less justified. Apparently, then, a combination of conservative and economic self-interest concerns triggered the uprising. Never before, said the head of the UFT, had supervisors and teachers acted with such unanimity. One lesson to be learned from all this is that the supervisory staff have considerable influence. Both the assistant superintendent and the principal are key figures at the local grassroots level.

Such tactics on the part of supervisors and teachers tend to reinforce the cynicism and alienation of militant civil rights leaders. The teachers claim that promises have been broken since the first attempts in the mid-1950's to integrate the schools. They have responded by making stronger demands on Dr. Gross, accompanied by threats of boycott or of withdrawal from negotiations. These threats exert pressures on those who wish to restrain such behavior and hold together a working consensus.

The next series of negotiating sessions with Dr. Gross covered school budgets. Civil rights groups recognized this as a key area of decision-making on which they would have to exercise pressure if they were to influence the speed and course of school integration. When negotiations on this subject first began, civil rights leaders claimed that over half the schools scheduled to be built from 1965 to 1971 were in ghetto or segregated areas. Dr. Gross agreed that the building program should be changed and said he was prepared to go to the Board of Education and even the Board of Estimate, if necessary. He agreed to the criterion that any future building plans should be dropped if they did not contribute to or detract from integration. He further agreed to operate as though there were no previously stated or established school or Board policy on construction.

One issue that came up quite early in the capital budget negotiations was the status of some decisions and the criteria for deciding which of them were too well advanced to reverse. More specifically, 38 schools were to be built in the fiscal year 1965-1966. It was still possible to relocate 23 of them. The negotiators considered this to be an indication of flexibility and good will on Dr. Gross's part.

Negotiating leaders remained divided throughout August. One faction took the position that the commitments Dr. Gross had made were the best so far in New York City, and that if they were carried out they would lead to substantially more integration. This group maintained that while they should bargain aggressively, they should also bargain in good faith and try to understand the problems of the school people. Their view was that if Dr. Gross's plans and commitments were not carried out, the responsibility for failure could be attributed to him and so publicized. However, his intentions seemed good and his commitments were more radical than anything in the preceding ten years. Some people asserted that since this is an imperfect world, not a utopia, the civil rights groups should be satisfied with the changes, even if they seemed less than speedy and radical. The final public statement of a plan, formulated at the end of August and signed at an open board meeting by all civil groups, was a serious test for this bargaining group. It contained a minimum of change, even by the standards of some moderate groups, in order to keep many undecided white middle class parents committed to the city's public school system. This first group in the civil rights-white liberal camp might be labeled the pragmatists.

A second point of view expressed by ideologists was uncertainty of the integrity of Dr. Gross. They were not sure that he meant what he was promising in the meetings, and they suspected that even if he did, the white establishment (UPA, PEA, and others) would force him to renege on the agreements he had made as too radical, irresponsible, and not taking into account the quality of education.

Several members of the Board of Education were disturbed that Dr. Gross developed such a close relationship with the civil rights leaders. He was subjected to pressure from such moderate groups as PEA and UPA as well as from some Board members to dissociate himself from identification with civil rights groups. He responded by asking them to think seriously about increasing the size of these meetings to include PEA, CCC, UPA, ADA, ADL, AJC, all traditional educational and intergroup organizations in the city and many embued with the spirit of social reform. When this issue was raised at the August 24 meeting of the Conference, the only agreement with Dr. Gross's revised point of view was expressed by one representative, who remarked that many like himself had been in operation much longer than the Conference, which could not possibly represent all the traditional views. He went on to state that if Dr. Gross met only with militant groups, this would polarize the sides once more and bring integration efforts to an unfortunate halt. It was most important for Gross to increase his communications with all groups in the community.

The proposal to enlarge the negotiating body was rejected by the Conference. It was noted first that Dr. Gross himself had made the original commitment to restrict the sessions to that limited group. Second, it would be very difficult to maintain the rapport established with Gross if other groups were invited. Third, but closely related to the second point, it was difficult enough to maintain the working consensus developed in a very small group. If more groups were added, the present working arrangements might break down. The Intergroup Committee was cited as a dramatic illustration of how political effectiveness could be hampered by too many members with diverse points of view. Finally, since the Conference already represented the groups Dr. Gross had suggested, why double the representation?

A compromise proposal involved holding some larger, periodic briefings of all citywide groups with the Board as an activity apart from the closed negotiating sessions. Since the public had been so uninformed about many Board policies, this was an opportunity to correct one defect of the system while at the same time satisfying the need to include a larger representation of community groups.

The negotiations of the Conference with Dr. Gross were basic to the future course of school integration in New York City, not only in terms of the specific policies and general programs that evolved but also because of the relationships that were established and the reactions of influentials who were not included to the legitimacy of the representation of negotiating parties. The civil rights-white liberal coalition is the most effective one to be assembled in the eleven-year history of integration activity in

New York City.   Like most coalitions in New York City politics,
however, it is tenuous.   Leaders of the coalition are unwilling
to predict its longevity.   Some members feel that the time of
greatest cohesion was in the fall of 1963, when the Board and Dr.
Gross were at odds, and also shortly thereafter, when the Board
announced plans for thirty pairings (January 31, 1964).   Others
consider this cohesion dubious in view of the deep-seated disagreements within the group over policy.   Furthermore, since
several leadership styles are likely to persist within the civil
rights movement for some time to come, with each interpreting
the needs and exigencies of the movement differently, long-term
cohesion seems unlikely.

Apparently any strong indications that the white community
is making major concessions and changes, even if they fall short
of expectations, lead to increased cohesion.   This happened just
before the first Negro boycott and later after the Allen Report,
although the situations were perceived differently.   Whenever
there is lack of cooperation by the white community, a split
occurs between the militant ideologists and the pragmatists, as,
for instance, at the time of the second boycott and again in July,
when evidence of supervisory tactics were uncovered in the Bronx.

Civil rights leaders were under extreme pressure to produce a plan, almost any plan, regardless of its educational feasibility, to professional educators and moderates.   They had to
show both constituents and skeptics some quick victories and
concessions if the coalition was to stay alive.   Dr. Gross, on
the other hand, had other publics with which to concern himself.
He had somehow to avoid alienating either the establishment or
the Mayor, since they were generally in agreement with liberal
leaders on the goals of better racial balance and upgrading the
quality of education.   But the Conference had to avoid extreme
criticism of the educational system and the white power structure
if it was to continue to gain concessions.   It is possible that the
right combination of events will produce both an absence of polarization on a citywide basis, continued communication among
groups holding different views, some flexible negotiation and bargaining, and orderly and fairly accelerated change.   This situation suggests the need for some kind of transactional model of
the requisites for change and administrative effectiveness in
school integration efforts.

THE PAT BOYCOTT

The second major strategy deployed is the boycott. Three major boycotts were used in 1964. The first was organized by the Negro civil rights groups in February, the second by the dynamic Rev. Milton Galamison, the Parents' Workshop and the Harlem Parents in March, both before the period involved in this field study. The third was a counterboycott staged by the white PAT and the Brooklyn Joint Council in September. Since this last boycott occurred during the study period, it is covered here in some detail as a manifest strategy used by those who wish to be heard and to prevail in the integration controversy but who have limited access to the core.

One of the most basic concerns of both PAT and the Joint Council was to preserve a situation of free choice or voluntarism for parents as to where to send their children to school. They opposed any compulsory transfer of pupils, white or Negro. In their more polemic statements PAT spokesmen referred to the dictatorial and totalitarian methods used by Dr. Gross and the Board in attempts to integrate the schools. They argued that they did not oppose integration at all, and that in fact they had contributed their services in previous integration plans, such as open enrollment. The argument about preserving freedom and voluntary free choice for parents, and its corollary, that the government and public agencies like school boards were usurping too much power and were engaged in compulsory programs that encroached on citizen rights, were generalized into an attempt to halt what they called the main drift of American life. The counterargument--that the Board had been making major educational decisions about zoning, curricula, and the like for years and that they should continue to do so, both as the voice of the broadest possible public interest and because of their greater educational competence--never was accepted by PAT and Joint Council followers. However, it certainly was not revolutionary for the Board to decide which schools children would attend.

It was argued that the preservation of neighborhood schools would provide people with a sense of community which they would lose under the Board's present integration plans. Indeed, it was charged that such plans as pairing would have a disintegrating effect on families and communities. Parents would be obliged to send their children to different schools and would have less time and energy to devote to Parents' Associations. It would be very difficult to have any sense of identification or involvement with a school that was far away. Furthermore, a mother would not be able to accompany each of her children to school so easily as in the past, since they would go in different directions. Older children would no longer be able to accompany younger siblings to school. Families and local neighborhoods would be broken up by such integration plans. Some of the more articulate spokesmen for this neighborhood school concept went on to point out that it had been the established doctrine for educators for several generations. Why should teachers or parents suddenly have to change their outlook on such a basic issue?

Another argument was that the quality of education for white middle-class children would decline if they were integrated with Negro children in pairings or educational park arrangements. Since there were no empirical data to substantiate this argument, the anxieties of some white parents could not be dispelled by Board representatives. As a matter of fact, UPA claimed to have data suggesting that Negro children bused in under the open enrollment plan were generally six months behind the white children in the receiving schools. This was interpreted as having the likely effect of lowering the level of the white children's instruction. Furthermore, since Negro pupils whose parents chose to send them to predominantly white schools under open enrollment were generally more advanced in IQ, reading level, and general academic achievement than their peers who remained in the ghetto schools, the quality of education would become even poorer under pairing and middle school plans.

It is essential to recognize that the arguments of PAT followers often masked even more basic needs that are difficult to express publicly. There are both public and private ideologies that must be distinguished in order to understand the dynamics of the PAT movement. One of the most basic underlying feelings is an acute sense of panic and anxiety. Some of this is simply the opposition to change that characterizes any conservative population. Earlier generations were hostile to succeeding waves of ethnic minority immigrants. Just as businessmen, anxious to preserve their property rights and managerial prerogatives, reacted to the increased demands and rights of labor, those elite groups who enjoyed a clear advantage over others had a vested interest in preserving the status quo. The social situation favored them and they intended to keep it that way.

The resistance to most recent Negro demands for rights and opportunities previously denied them seems to differ, however, in both degree and kind from previous reactions. Now the panic stems from anticipating where school integration will lead. The conservatives fear that the Board has some long-run plans and timetables that will involve mass busing of many more white children. They fear that contact with Negro children will acquaint white children with less desirable ways of life. They fear that more white children will be forcibly bused into squalid Negro neighborhoods. They fear that school integration ultimately will encourage Negro families to move into white neighborhoods, bringing with them the same lowering of property values and local deterioration that has been experienced in Brooklyn, the East Bronx, and other areas of the city. Finally, they fear that increased social contact between Negro and white children eventually will lead to intermarriage and a lowering of the quality of the white race. Underlying all these fears is an extreme sense of resentment against the system for forcing such changes on the white community without allowing for any negotiation, compromise, or democratic dialogue for the expression of community sentiment. The refusal of the Mayor or the City Council to grant a simple referendum on school integration plans, methods of recruitment to school boards, or other educational matters was cited as indicative of how the system overrode the white community.

The first organized effort of the school integration opponents was a PAT-organized protest march and demonstration on City Hall and the Board on March 13, 1964. This was in response to a successful show of strength by the Negro February and March boycotts. News reporters estimated that as many as 15,000 parents, mostly women, turned out for the occasion, despite adverse weather conditions. The leaders held meetings with Dr. Gross, Board President James Donovan, City Council President Paul R. Screvane, and Deputy Mayor Edward F. Cavanagh, Jr., but they received no satisfaction on any occasion. Obviously this was an extremely well-organized movement, one that could not be disregarded. All through the spring and early summer months responsible civil rights leaders warned the white community of the threat to its integration plans from the PAT-Joint Council group. They reiterated that there was a leadership vacuum among moderate groups in New York City, as there was in many southern communities, and that unless the responsible white groups spoke up much more vigorously for integration and provided some leadership, the opposition group (PAT-Joint Council) would flourish. The result could be to set back integration efforts for many years.

The NAACP and more militant Negro point of view defined the situation as a white problem that must be met by white, not Negro, leadership. Since PAT appealed primarily, indeed overwhelmingly, to the white community, it was the task of responsible community leaders to speak out not against boycotts per se but against PAT and what it stood for. The situation was seen, then, as a white problem and as an opportunity for whites to take a stand.

The first concerted strategy of the parents group was to attempt to win over the Board and Dr. Gross to their point of view in private meetings with Dr. Gross and at various open meetings of the Board. Dr. Gross aroused their anger almost to fever pitch as he informed them that the integration plan was an accomplished fact and that if there were to be any changes in the plan they would take effect in September, 1965.

This action, of course, shut him off from any bargaining relationship with PAT and Joint Council leaders. His strategy for handling the latter was to mobilize as large a coalition behind his program as possible, hoping thus to minimize his opposition. Since PAT-Joint Council requests for an end to Board transfer plans, changes in school boundaries, and other measures were unacceptable even to many moderate groups, Dr. Gross had no choice but to stand by the plans he had evolved in negotiating sessions with liberal leaders. He realized that any attempt at bargaining and compromise with PAT and Joint Council leaders would be political suicide. His main hope was that the moderate groups would sway enough potential opponents of the plans so that the opposition movement itself would subside.

Gross did receive some help from the moderates. As early as June 5, Dr. Frederick C. McLaughlin, Executive Director of PEA, declared:

> The plan provides a basis for moving forward. All groups should now close ranks behind the Superintendent and his staff and help, where possible, in securing resources for the implementation of the new program. Such support in no way limits future

action. Continued opposition, however, endangers
not only education but our whole democratic process.[1]

Both the PEA and the UPA regarded their roles as those of maintaining continued communications with opposition groups at a
time when it seemed that such communications were impossible
for any other citywide groups. Even though rank-and-file Negro
parents were not as militant as some of their leaders, there certainly was pressure on leaders to make some progress after
what were considered ten years of extremely limited success.

    The repeated failures of integration opponents in their at-
tempts to deal directly with the Board were followed by a summer of legal battles. Three influential PAT leaders were lawyers.
They brought six suits against the Board of Education, attacking
the constitutionality of the pairings for the fall of 1964. They
lost five of the suits. Their argument was that the Board could
not force children, solely on the basis of color, to attend schools
outside their neighborhoods. They maintained that zoning could
not be based on racial factors. Though PAT lawyers were willing
to admit that de facto segregation existed and that it was undesirable, they charged that the problem must be attacked in other
ways, for instance, through changes in housing patterns. The
Board contended that the pairing was not planned solely for the
purpose of achieving greater racial balance. It was also intended
to upgrade the quality of education in both paired schools, e.g.,
to relieve overcrowding and make possible smaller classes and
improved services. All the cases were in paired areas--one in
Lincoln Towers, one in Long Island City, two in Jackson Heights,
and one in Brooklyn Heights. The one PAT victory was in Jackson Heights, where Justice Henry J. Latham ruled in July that
the Board could not transfer three white children from a school
across the street from their homes. However, the judge said
nothing to suggest the unconstitutionality of pairings as such.

    Another major court defeat for pairing foes occurred just
a few days before school opened. Justice Sidney A. Fine refused
to permit a citywide referendum on the Board's pairing plan.
The court based its rejection on the preeminence of the state in

---

[1]Leonard Buder in The New York Times, June 6, 1964, p. 1.

establishing educational policy and the lateness of the petition
seeking the referendum. Pairing foes had been working that summer to secure the necessary 30,000 signatures to make valid
their petition. For a number of reasons they had been unable to
convince the court that they had the necessary signatures until it
was almost too late to make a ruling for the fall. At one point
in July the City Clerk had questioned the legitimacy of some signatures, implying that they were from parents not involved in
the city's pairings or public school system.

Justice Fine based his ruling on the following arguments:
First, a recent decision of the Court of Appeals, the state's
highest tribunal, established a precedent in contending that the
Board of Education has "express statutory power to select a site
and to determine the school where each pupil shall attend."
As a result, Justice Fine said, "the proposed local law would
thus, in effect, supersede state statutes referred to by the Court
of Appeals" and be illegal under Article 9 of the State Constitution, which prohibits enactment of a local law over a state law.
Second, he ruled that the petition had been filed too late for the
November 3 election.

One tactic attempted by Bernard Kessler, who represented
PAT in most court suits, involved invoking the Civil Rights Act
against Board pairings. This maneuver was tried in a suit
against the PS 111-112 (Long Island City) pairing. The move
was rejected. The law states that "desegregation shall not mean
the assignment of students to public schools in order to overcome
racial imbalance." Justice Nicholas M. Pette refused to accept
this provision of the law as any basis for ruling against pairings.
To accept the PAT contention that the Civil Rights Act would
negate the Board's pairings would transmute that act into a segregation law when its clear import was antisegregation.

Justice Pette's summary statement probably set the precedent for future court cases. He observed that other cases on
the constitutionality of pairings already had been tried and ruled
in the Board's favor. The main argument in the Board's defense
was that the reduction of racial imbalance was not the most important factor in its decision to pair. Rather, the pairings had
contributed to an upgrading of the quality of education in each
school, thereby permitting substantially reduced class sizes,
additional professional services, and other educational advantages
as well as offering an early opportunity for children to live and

work together in a multiracial setting. Thus, the Board had been so circumspect in its final pairing plans, having decided against many others, and it was so careful to provide an incentive each time, that no convincing case could be made in opposition. PAT lawyers still plan more contests, however, pursuing a different line of argument. Instead of concentrating on the constitutionality of pairings, rezoning, and new middle schools, PAT lawyers will challenge such plans on the ground that they are educationally unsound.

Having lost, then, in its attempts to negotiate either directly with the Board or through the courts, the opposition turned to Mayor Wagner and the City Council for help. At first Mayor Wagner made himself unavailable, stating that educational matters must be kept out of politics and decided by educational professionals. The opposition threatened to demonstrate at the Democratic National convention in Atlantic City, where Wagner was being considered for the Vice Presidential nomination. In fact, they exerted pressure on members of both conventions to include in their party platform a provision upholding the neighborhood school. Mayor Wagner finally met with them in September in an attempt to temper their emotions. He handled this situation as he had many others in his long service as Mayor. First, he told the group that he was powerless to interfere, because the Board of Education was a semi-autonomous agency under state jurisdiction. He sought to rely on court decisions to avoid being pushed into exerting direct influence himself. The courts, as well as the authority of the State Board of Education, the Board of Regents, and the legislature thus could help him out of his predicament. Since Wagner was playing this issue to a national as well as citywide audience, he wanted to maintain an image of not catering to extremists. Therefore he would not yield to the PAT-Joint Council pleas. He also promised to study the situation and speak with members of the Board, but this delaying tactic was perceived as such. The PAT-Joint Council people were especially bitter about the Mayor's failure to act when Council Minority Leader Angelo J. Arculeo (Republican) of Brooklyn and four other Councilmen had petitioned him on August 18 to call a special session of the Council to consider four pieces of anticompulsory integration legislation. Arculeo claimed that the New York City Charter stipulated that the Mayor was required to call such a session upon receipt of the signatures of five Councilmen. "By his illegal refusal to call a special meeting," Arculeo charged, "he is depriving the people of their right to have their elected representatives heard before the Board's disastrous plan is put into effect."[1] Arculeo vowed to sue the Mayor and went so far as to call on Corporation Counsel Larkin to force Wagner to convene a special session of the City Council before the schools opened.

In early August, when it became clear to PAT-Joint Council leaders that they would not win either in the courts or through direct negotiations with Dr. Gross and the Board, they decided to stage a massive white boycott of public schools on opening day. They may have assumed that the Board could be swayed as it had been after the Negro boycotts of February and March. They may also have assumed that such a demonstration would force the Mayor to move, knowing as they did his strategy of negotiating a deal at the critical eleventh hour. At any rate, most of the public discussion and influence-wielding from August 10 through the opening of school related to the proposed boycott.

A main target of PAT attacks in preparation for the boycott was Mayor Wagner, rather than Dr. Gross and the Board. An attempt was made to single out the Mayor for blame, thus trying to force him to intervene. As Frederick Reuss, Queens PAT leader, declared:

> Mayor Wagner and his political cronies, by refusing to listen to the voice of the people or to consult with representatives of the majority of the people, have made it necessary for PAT to take this step. He will either have to represent the people or step down from his high office in order that the people may be represented by a man more willing and able to understand the problems of this city. [2]

The boycott was portrayed as a democratic protest by a majority of the populus whose interest heretofore had been denied.

PAT leaders hoped to use the threatened boycott to negotiate with Dr. Gross and the Board. They offered to cancel the boycott if the Board would cancel its four pairings. They ex-

---

[1] New York Post, September 10, 1964.
[2] The New York Times, August 11, 1964.

pressed willingness to abide by all other voluntary integration plans, such as open enrollment, an offer which they felt clearly demonstrated their lack of prejudice. The Board, of course, refused to engage in any negotiations to weaken its already modest plans. Therefore, PAT considered all meetings with the Mayor unsatisfactory in dealing with the real issues, and they continued with their preparations.

The Board and Dr. Gross, on the other hand, embarked on an intensive public relations program in an attempt to mobilize as much citizen consensus behind their plan as possible. Liberal critics of the Board and Dr. Gross, while pleased with such a spirited defense of the integration program, were concerned that its formulation had taken so long. Any politically sound program, they argued, should have planned for a longer term effort to gain citizen acceptance.

In anticipation of widespread support for the Board's plans from many groups, PAT-Joint Council leaders developed a counterstrategy, hoping to keep or win back white parent followers. On September 8 they suddenly limited their plan for a school boycott of what had previously been declared indefinite duration. Instead, they asked parents throughout the city to keep their children out of school for just the two opening days of the new term, September 14 and 15, except for those pupils who were involuntarily transferred and would remain out until they were again admitted to neighborhood schools. [1] In order to gain greater parent acceptance, the statement said that the withdrawal would have no adverse educational effect, for practically no school work would be begun until after the Yom Kippur holiday on September 16.

PAT-Joint Council preparations for the boycott indicated the effectiveness of their organization. Many white parents in Queens, Brooklyn, and the Bronx, who previously had not participated in such activities, willingly volunteered their help in preparing pamphlets, making phone calls, and doing other tasks to mobilize the largest possible following. Many of these women had no other interests or activities, and the boycott provided meaning in their lives. One editorialist wryly observed, "If this much personnel, time, and energy were redirected to actually improving the quality of education for all children, we would have much to look forward to for New York City's public school system."[2]

---

[1]The New York Times, September 8, 1964.
[2]New York Post, editorial, September 6, 1964.

Meanwhile, Dr. Gross and selected representatives of the Board were busy presenting their plan to the community. Negro civil rights leaders did not participate directly, for they considered this as a white parents' movement that must be countered by white parents. EQUAL played a major role, attempting to hold neighborhood meetings for parents at which the Board's plans were explained, sending out notices and pleas to white parents throughout the city, attempting to influence opinion leaders in local areas, and finally appearing on television in dramatic, last-minute requests to white parents to send their children to school. They also conducted the silent vigil referred to by Mrs. Lurie outside the day school hastily set up in the basement of a cooperative apartment building in Jackson Heights.

In addition, all the moderate groups openly opposed the boycott. One of the most significant groups in terms of political power was the UPA, which represented 400,000 parents in Parents' Associations throughout the city. Both the CCC and PEA issued strong statements against the boycott. Most of the statements announced that these groups were against the principle of boycotting and, as so many said, "of using the children as pawns in adult struggles." There was a conspicuous absence of statements to the effect that these groups opposed this particular boycott because it represented an unwillingness to accept an even modest integration program and therefore condoned a continuation of de facto segregation.

James B. Donovan, Board President, appeared on television to defend the Board and its plans. Donovan inflamed the opposition by threatening the boycotting parents with legal sanctions. The most forceful statement of all came when Dr. Gross made a fifteen-minute television appearance shortly before the schools were to open. This was a taped telecast that was repeated many times that evening. Gross's statement was the strongest to be made by a school official. The main theme was that New Yorkers had been treated to a barrage of inflammatory statements that simply were not true and that the city needed to clear the air with the facts. He charged that many false and misleading statements had been made by PAT leaders, who said that there would be many more future pairings. Gross called their predictions silly and fantastic. He berated the PAT leaders for urging parents to break the law by using their children as pawns in a reprehensible power play. He effectively attempted to dispel the many rumors that were so rampant, appealed to law and order, and asked for cooperation with the Board's plans. Most important, he stressed the limited amount of extra busing involved in the new plan and the considerable attention given to upgrading the quality of educational services in paired schools. He spoke about his goal of better schools for all children to preserve community solidarity and upgrade the educational opportunities for children from ghetto areas.

Dr. Gross explained all the facets of the plan in great detail, underlining the fact that this was a modest beginning. He stated emphatically that the Board believed in the principles of maintaining a democratic society and implied that this was not the belief of opposition groups.

Boycott plans were too far advanced by now, however, for any last-minute pleas to have much impact. It was apparent to all moderate and liberal groups that PAT-Joint Council leaders were very well organized, had an abundance of personnel and finances, and were prepared to fight the Board's program to the end.

Despite the last-minute efforts of Mayor Wagner, who responded characteristically in such a crisis with efforts at mediation, the boycott took place during the first two days of school. Dr. Gross, Jacob Landers, the Assistant Superintendent for Integration, PEA officials, Mrs. Ellen Lurie of EQUAL, UPA leaders, and others all had urged parents in paired areas and elsewhere to send their children to school.

On the first day 275,638 pupils stayed home, a figure that was 175,000 over the normal 10 per cent absence rate. One school, PS 112 in the Bensonhurst section of Brooklyn, was empty, despite the fact that it was not involved in any pairing and was quite far away from schools that were. As one parent from this school put it: "We know that eventually the Board of Education will come down to our school with its plans." Though this unusual case was not repeated anywhere else in the city, it did serve to dramatize the fear and anxiety of many white parents for the future. Certainly these fears were continually intensified by PAT and Joint Council leaders. Most surprising in the PS 112 situation was the fact that the principal was completely unaware of the effect of the impending boycott. The principal, a man who had spent 26 years in the school system, very much favored integration, and seemed to have the support of parents in his community, said he was stunned by the total absence record in his school.

CONCLUSION

It is obvious that the use of certain strategies depends on the three factors--size, distance, and time--which relate the positions of the core and constellations of satellite groups in the educational arena, as discussed in Chapter III. The leadership dialogue was initiated by the Superintendent at a time when the Board had adopted a policy and he was relatively free to engage in meetings with community groups to clarify the meaning of the plans and establish channels of communications. His interest was that the policy be better understood and the likelihood of community controversy be reduced. Of course, the civil rights groups, appreciative of the opportunity to express themselves, viewed the sessions as a means of moving much closer to the center of authority and at the same time entering the session as a place to negotiate and bargain on future integration policy.

Generally several factors operate to make a leadership dialogue effective. One is that all points of view are represented and articulated. Second, there is some assurance that the leaders actually do represent specific constituents to the dispute in the community. Third, the participants should be willing to listen to the views of others. Fourth, there is sufficient motivation and good will to gain a degree of consensus in order that some mutually decided policy or action can proceed. Fifth, there should be good staff work in preparation for the meetings so that the participants have had an opportunity to prepare for the sessions. Finally, the objectives of the dialogue should be attainable. Most of these conditions, however, were absent from the dialogue. Only the civil rights groups were present, thus precluding the operation of the other factors.

The exclusion from the leadership dialogue of those opposed to specific integration proposals stimulated the development of the boycott as a strategy to force the core group to take the objections seriously. PAT, remote from the center of authority, propitiously chose the opening of school for a large-scale dramatic demonstration by white parents in the community of their opposition to school policies. The surprisingly large proportion in support of the boycott impressed school officials and political figures alike. The Mayor insisted that the Superintendent meet with PAT representatives, but little effort was made to include them in the leadership dialogue, for the bipolarization of the contending factions made it improbable that they could reach a working consensus. The meaning and significance of the boycott still is unclear in the literature of the social sciences, although it has become an increasingly popular strategy in the civil rights movement. In the next chapter an effort will be made to understand this strategy as a measure of white parent decision-making.

Chapter 7

MEASURING WHITE PARENT
DECISIONS ON SCHOOL PAIRING

INTRODUCTION

Racial integration of the public schools in large northern cities is one of the most dramatic kinds of social change in America today. No other issue has disturbed New York City in the way or to the degree that the school integration controversy has during the past few years. In fact, New Yorkers are discovering nerves they never knew they had and muscles they have seldom tried.

Integration is a citywide issue, unlike slum clearance, for example, since the school populations in all neighborhoods are involved, whereas urban renewal affects relatively smaller areas and less powerful groups of citizens. Also, northerners have no clearly developed, realistic ideas of what an integrated society implies for their daily lives--at school, at home, and at work-- for so far they have been only spectators or members of the cheering sections while events have been occurring in the remote South. The issue of school integration now is forcing many people to make individual, group, and community decisions that they have not anticipated.

The reason for the furor surrounding school integration is the policy dispute over the use of the public school as an agent of social change. The fact that the public school plays a significant part in integrating and molding American society should be no surprise. One of the school's historic functions, almost from the beginning, has been to assimilate the waves of immigrants coming to America, particularly to New York City. What is surprising is that our own generation finds itself in such disagreement over the role of the school.

The dispute has two parts. The first is to decide <u>what</u> function the public schools shall perform in integrating our

---

[1]Revised version of paper delivered to the American Education Research Association, Chicago, Ill., February 12, 1965.

society and reversing or counteracting the many private decisions that have established a de facto segregated housing pattern. The school is being asked to transform community life and reduce, if not eliminate, the vast social distance separating whites and Negroes. This demand stems from the assumption that the school is a place of equal opportunity, where everyone can acquire the skills needed in a democratic society. Education has become a prerequisite to mobility and a principal means of climbing the ladder to success. Therefore, middle class whites seek access to the best public schools. They have a long tradition of voicing their demands for better schools and in fact often view schools as their property. Many integration proposals find them zealously guarding against any diminution of the quality education they demand and expect. School integration appears to threaten them with surrender of their hard-won share of scarce educational resources and services to a group that has made few effective demands in the past. The whites fear that integration will downgrade the public schools, lessen educational opportunities for their children, and enhance the struggle to enter the colleges that are the pathway to the material success awaiting all Americans with good educations.

There is, then, a basic conflict between two American values. One is the belief in equality of opportunity; the other is the strong need for individual achievement, mobility, and success. Integration has brought both into focus, thus highlighting the competitive tensions that challenge assumptions about the democratic role of schools in our society and the particular integrative function they should perform.

The second part of the integration dispute is who shall decide public school policies. The integration issue has brought forth many contenders who seek to prevail over school policy-making. Without listing them all, we wish to examine the relationships between those who formulate citywide policy at the top level and those on the local school level who are most affected by these decisions. More specifically, we are concerned with the interplay of forces between central headquarters and the subcommunity or local school area and in how participants at both levels interact to shape integration policy. There are 25 school districts within the city, each with its own local school board (LSB) of lay leaders and administrative staff of field superintendents. There is no reason to assume that those at the top level completely dominate what should be and what actually is done at the local level, or the converse, that those on the local level refuse to implement citywide policy objectives. Rather, we ask who prevails on what plan, and when and where it will be used.

This chapter records the initial efforts to identify some of the relevant factors in the exercise of power and influence in school policy-making. During this past year observations were made of school "pairing" controversies in New York City with the objectives of constructing a political map of the system and evaluating data availability. This is a report on the exploratory phase intended to develop a specific measure of local citizen and parent response to selected integration policies. The research budget precludes a survey of citizen and parent attitudes and behavior. Therefore, the manifest and aggregate behavior, such as demonstrations and attendance records, will be relied upon as reflecting community and parent response to pairing. To be sure, these rather crude measures do not identify what kinds of people are responding in what ways from what sets of backgrounds, beliefs, and experiences. Yet, aggregate data are available and their utility is being evaluated. An early reading will develop the power relationships between those who formulate citywide policy and parents who are most directly affected at the local level.

SCHOOL PAIRING

School pairing is the major focus of this attempt to measure white parent decisions. It provides an excellent setting in which to examine the power relationships between the New York City School Board and the local school areas. Pairing was the most controversial aspect of the 1964 integration plan, for it represented a major shift from the voluntary integration plans of the past. Pairing follows the nonvoluntary principle of rezoning and is designed to integrate those schools along the critical fringe areas of ghettos. The Princeton Plan has gained national recognition as a workable scheme to integrate northern schools where de facto segregation exists. The plan involves a simple technique of abolishing school boundary zones and assigning students to schools outside their immediate neighborhoods. This method breaks down the segregated school by combining neighborhoods that have become ethnic enclaves. While the idea of pairing was conceived and initiated in a small town, it is believed workable also in New York City. The boundaries of two neighboring elementary schools would be joined together to comprise one new

104

school district or area. Each school would retain its own kindergarten class for those youngsters living in the immediate neighborhood. The other grades would be interchanged to make each part of the other. In one case a single principal now administers both schools.

The civil rights groups suggested that some 80 to one hundred sets of schools be paired, but they presented no specific plan nor did they identify particular schools. In the fall of 1963 the Superintendent surveyed local school administrative officials and community groups to determine what could be done to increase the integration of the schools in each district.

The local field superintendents were imaginative in suggesting a great variety of proposals. These included recommendations to: establish heterogeneous classes; develop "buddy" schools for intervisitations, correspondence, joint festivals, assemblies, and the like; install portable classrooms in the yards of white schools; change zones; stress ethnic contributions to American life in the curriculum; conduct a series of human relations workshops for parents and teachers, and many similar plans. At the same time the administrative staff began to examine the number, location, and form these pairings should take.

The pairing of predominantly white PS 149 in Jackson Heights with virtually all-Negro PS 92 in Corona served as a model for the 1964 pairing proposal. The PA's of both schools thought their area was ready to participate in the program, since they were assured by the Board of Education that class size would be reduced and the minority school would be renovated. The PA's negotiated for and received additional personnel totaling $82,345. including reading specialists, librarian, guidance counselor, social worker, psychologist, psychiatrist, doctor, and nurses. But the New York Herald Tribune's announcement that the area was scheduled for pairing took many parents by surprise. Reaction was violent as substantial numbers of them, heretofore inactive in PA and community affairs, formed the now-famous Parents and Taxpayers Association (PAT). Nevertheless, leaders of the PA and the LSB upheld their commitment to participate in the pairing, even after lengthy public hearings and increasing community controversy. Their resolute stand served to intensify the opposition, which soon became a citywide movement to protect others whose neighborhood schools were threatened. The School Board assigned two central headquarters units--Human Relations and Central Zoning--to serve as consultants to the local area and created a new Superintendency on Integration.

The controversy grew, and on February 3 the Negroes and Puerto Ricans staged a citywide school boycott, pulling out about half the student body. A repetition of the boycott on March 3 was less successful, for now the Negro leadership was split into factions supporting and opposing the move. Caught between the pressures of a militant civil rights movement and the blistering attack by a rapidly growing PAT, the Superintendent of Schools held an intensive week-long series of discussions with the LSB's and his administrative staff at both the local and top levels to select the sets of schools to be paired. The conditions of some 26 of the elementary school pairings were reviewed, with attention being given not only to the criteria of integration and other zoning principles but also to the predicted degree of community acceptance. Nine of these schools were "sending" schools (minority) and six were "receiving" schools (white) in the open enrollment program and therefore had already had some direct experience with integration activities. All except four had been losing their proportions of whites--an essential ingredient for integration--during the previous five years, one by as much as 70 per cent. All except three minority schools had less than 25 per cent white pupils, while all except seven of the white schools comprised over 75 per cent whites. Queens, with 13 schools, was the borough most affected, followed by Brooklyn with seven, Manhattan with only three, and the Bronx with two.

Some of the proposed pairings were postponed or eliminated after the hearing of arguments that included local community hostility, fear of losing the teaching staff, the need for improved transportation facilities, and the feeling that other alternatives might work better and produce greater integration. After months of study, appraisal, and negotiation, the Board of Education announced four full pairings and one partial or one-grade-a-year pairing for the academic year beginning in September, 1964. Other programs such as transferring sixth graders into junior high school, changes in the feeder patterns to junior and senior high schools, and special services schools were announced at the same time. While pairing became the major policy change, it involved only a small fraction of the pupils in the segregated elementary schools. Yet pairing drew the most public attention, stirred up the deepest emotions, and provoked the greatest controversy and conflict in the community.

The opposition, directed mainly by the white PAT, was expressed at various levels of the polity, but most actively at the local school area level. Attempts were made, however, to affect city politics during the presidential campaign in which Republican candidate Barry Goldwater spoke against busing as did incumbent Senator Kenneth Keating and his opponent, Robert Kennedy. PAT leaders also sought to set aside the school order for pairing by appealing to the Republican-controlled State Legislature, the Democrat-controlled City Council, the Board of Education, the Office of the Mayor, and the National Democratic Convention--all without success. Yet President Lyndon Johnson piled up huge local majorities, two out of three votes in Queens, a conservative stronghold, and three out of four in Brooklyn.

PAT also contested each pairing and partial pairing in the courts. In each instance they lost, with the exception of three separate petitions in behalf of three children who claimed special hazards. One case may still go to the U.S. Supreme Court on appeal.

The lack of success in the political arena does not tell the full story, however, for it indicates only that public officials were able to set aside PAT complaints. School officials implemented only four full pairings instead of the hundred originally requested and the 26 so thoroughly studied.

Thus, while the policy decision to pair the schools was made by the New York City Board of Education, the real effect was felt at the local school area level. Each school selected for pairing either sought to modify the full impact of the plan or used it as an opportunity to bargain for more and improved educational services. Problems of transportation, building programs, and teacher resistance offered additional impediments. In other words, few schools willingly accepted pairing, for it represented a radical break with the traditional neighborhood school concept initiated and nurtured by school authorities.

An important part of understanding what happened in New York City this past year lies in assessing the white parent response at the local subcommunity level. We have available two measurable pieces of information about this response. The first is the attendance records for each school during the PAT-sponsored citywide boycott on September 14 and 15, 1964. The second is the parents' actual response as shown by classroom racial counts of those taking their assigned seats by October 31.

The Boycott

The schools in the boroughs of Queens and Brooklyn were most extensively considered for pairing, since many neighborhoods were undergoing racial migrations. These same neighborhoods also were experiencing considerable racial tensions over property values and the like. Here the racial concentrations and enclaves of minority families caused de facto segregated schools. It was here, then, in the most sensitive areas in the city, that the school officials decided to apply the pairing device. Thirty-seven sets of pairings were considered in these two boroughs,[1] and appeared to meet the following established criteria:

1. Ethnic composition of the schools to be involved must have a substantial differential in "others" category.

2. The distance from one building to the other should not be more than 1-1/2 miles.

3. The distance between the extreme boundaries of the schools involved should not be more than 2-1/2 miles or a travel time of 30 minutes.

Sixteen pairings were dropped during administrative deliberations, while 17 were considered very intensively through a weeklong series of hearings by the Superintendent of Schools with representatives from the local schools involved. These included not only administrative staff but members of the local school board and leaders of parent organizations. It is from this last list that the Board of Education decided to pair four sets of schools.

The schools with low attendance records during this boycott can logically be considered as resisting the integration plan. Indeed, the attendance record may be a better measure of

---

[1] Several pairings also were considered in Manhattan where one partial pairing was established and in the Bronx where no pairings were adopted.

parental decision on this question than the drama of community response on the picket lines as recorded by television and news cameramen. Our field observation during the boycott led us as well as the newsmen to believe that Jackson Heights in Queens was the most resisting area in the city. Certainly emotional tension was high, as was community unrest. Borough by borough, however, Brooklyn had the lowest attendance record (61.7 per cent), then Queens (69.1 per cent), the Bronx (74.6 per cent), Manhattan (82.7 per cent), and Richmond (91.3 per cent). A 90 per cent attendance record is considered normal.

More specifically, PS 149 had the highest boycott support on September 14 of the four sets of pairs. But it was by no means the most supportive school in the city. In fact, Table I shows that the parents of students in the publicly considered schools were more supportive of the boycott, and that those schools considered administratively were the least.

TABLE I

Brooklyn and Queens School Attendance
During September 15 Boycott

Attendance Per Cent	Administrative Consideration		Public Consideration		Paired	
	No.	Per Cent	No.	Per Cent	No.	Per Cent
0-20	--	--	5	28.0	--	--
21-40	3	18.8	6	35.3	--	--
41-60	2	12.5	4	21.1	2	50.0
61-80	3	18.8	2	15.6	2	50.0
81-100	8	50.0	--	--	--	--

While the number of paired schools is small, one can speculate that those schools that had been publicly considered but were not paired either were wisely excluded by the Board or responsively listened to by school officials as the parents involved effectively demonstrated their disapproval. Another explanation may be that the educational and community conditions

in the paired schools--particularly in PS 112 in Queens and PS 8
in Brooklyn, which were the more accepting schools, with 71 and
76 per cent attendance records respectively--were satisfactory
enough to avoid large-scale resistance. Both local PA's involved
approved the PS 8 plan and even demonstrated before Central
School Headquarters in favor of the plan.

The Racial Count

The second measure is the parents' decisions to reject the
plan or to accept it and send children to their assigned places in
the paired schools. This information comes in the form of the
"racial counts" made by each classroom teacher on October 31,
1964, and can be used as a check against the boycott support and
the proportion of whites who did not return to school. It should
be pointed out, however, that two different kinds of decisions are
expressed here. To boycott on the opening days of school is a
momentary protest against top leaders and their policies. On
the other hand, not to accept an assigned place implies withdrawal from the school system and a decision of far greater con-
sequence than a temporary protest.

The racial count data two months after school began indicates that the white parents of PS 148 in East Elmhurst were
the most resisting. They not only refused to send 180 of their
children to the minority school (PS 127)--a discrepancy of 11.6
per cent from the expected ratio of whites--but they refused to
send 121 of their children to the neighborhood school (PS 148)--
a discrepancy of 12.2 per cent. Jackson Heights parents, on the
other hand, enrolled their children in the predominantly white
neighborhood school as expected. However, they refused to send
102 children to the minority school (PS 92).

Table II shows the discrepancy between the proportion of
whites anticipated to attend each school and planned for by school
officials and the actual racial count. Some of this discrepancy
may show a normal rate of movement by families from one
neighborhood to another. Some may be due to a few rezonings to
make more room for smaller classes. These kind of data are
not presently available.

TABLE II

Proportions of White Attendance
in the Four Sets of School Pairings

School	Registration	September Boycott Attendance %	Expected "Other" Paired Attendance #	Expected "Other" Paired Attendance %	October 31 "Other" Racial Count #	October 31 "Other" Racial Count %	Rate of Discrepancy
PS 149 Q	846	42.0	649	74.8	623	75.3	+ .9
92 Q	488	52.7	295	52.8	193	40.7	-12.1
148 Q	587	53.5	581	74.1	454	61.9	-12.2
127 Q	1047	56.5	548	52.7	368	41.4	-11.6
112 Q	647	71.1	450	61.4	302	48.6	-12.8
111 Q	846	73.3	503	57.3	388	49.9	- 7.4
8 B	667	76.0	325	48.8	248	42.2	- 6.6
7 B	291	82.8	98	31.5	76	22.6	- 8.9

Q - Queens
B - Brooklyn

Something more must be known about the character of the plan as it was applied to each pairing, as well as something about the changing educational environment and practice to which the parents were expected to adjust. Table III indicates that PS 149 was the only paired white school asked to send the younger (first and second grade) students to the minority school. The upper grades were assigned to PS 149, for it had two gymnasiums while PS 92 had none, and upper grade students, of course, would make better use of these facilities. It is well recognized that it is more difficult for parents to accept sending their youngest children farther away to school. In all cases except PS 7 in Brooklyn the white children were expected to attend a school where they would be the distinct minority, while those who remained would form only about half the student body in their own neighborhood school. However, the fact that PS 7 was the only

111

TABLE III

Changes Planned for in Pairing

School	"Others" in 1963		"Others" After Pairing		Change* of "Others"		Grades	Greatest Distance Traveled	Number of Pupils Bused
	#	%	#	%	#	%			
PS 149	921	87.0	649	74.8	-272	-12.2	K, 3-6	.92 mi.	101
92	2	0.4	295	52.8	+293	+52.4	K-2		
148	1047	87.3	581	74.1	-466	-13.2	K-2	1.37 mi.	257
127	45	6.0	548	52.7	+503	+46.7	K, 3-6		
112	716	83.4	450	61.4	-266	-22.0	K-3	.96 mi.	135
111	230	22.1	503	57.3	+273	+35.2	K, 4-6		
8	360	77.3	325	48.8	-35	-28.5	K-4	1.4 mi.	519
7	17	3.6	98	31.5	+81	+27.9	K, 5-6		

*Discrepancies in numbers of students moved is due to other rezonings.

school with a sizable proportion of Puerto Ricans may have eased the transition.

The actual number of students involved is another important factor in accounting for resistance. Some 500 white children were expected to move from PS 148, whereas less than 300 were expected to move from PS 149 and PS 112, and only 35 students were moved from PS 8. These data suggest that the larger the number of families involved, the greater the probability of resistance, as PS 8 had much smaller numbers but a larger proportion of change and demonstrated the least resistance. The students in the PS 148-PS 127 pairing had the longest distance to travel and the most pupils bused.

Thus, PS 8 was proven by both measures to be more accepting of the plan than the areas involved in the other pairings. This may be due to the efforts made to gain community and parent acceptance and give the local school community a role in shaping the plan. It may be that the community characteristics of the two areas--PS 8 and PS 7--provide a sufficient condition for acceptance, since the pairing matched a middle class with a lower class area. Here social distance can be maintained, for there may be little contact in de facto segregated classrooms where the "track" system operates. It may also mean that PS 8 accepted pairing because the educational environment would be improved with additional services and smaller class size, yet these were provided for all paired schools. This may explain why the paired schools were less supportive than those considered for pairing. It may also be that some parents not only have accepted the principle of integration but are willing and prepared to have it become part of their own children's educational experience. In order to explore these possible reasons we need more cases for analysis and more information on families' decisions as they react to pairing and other integration plans.

IMPLICATIONS

This research thus far provides the basis for comments on the three issues: (1) pairing as one integration proposal; (2) the difficulty of implementing citywide policy at the local level; and (3) the search for measurable indices of community and parental acceptance. As already noted, these statements are tentative, for the project is in an early phase of constructing a political map of the school system and evaluating data availability.

Pairing is a definite break with past integration policies, for it uses a more drastic nonvoluntary effort to stem the tide of increasing numbers of segregated schools. The plan has been introduced in those critical fringe areas where either the minority and white neighborhoods are in transition or there is already a perceived threat to property values and a way of life. As should be expected, these are the very areas most sensitive to being paired. The fact that there were varying degrees of resistance requires further study of parent decisions, community attitudes, and the methods of introducing and implementing the integration plans by school officials.

In any event, the turn away from voluntary efforts has seriously challenged the democratic assumptions of many New Yorkers and created controversy over the function of the schools and the role of citizens in shaping this policy. Even though there will be no more pairing adopted in the immediate future, it symbolizes a turn away from the neighborhood school, developed and nurtured for many years by educational leaders. Current proposals will replace it by the "educational complex" and "educational park" which will draw students from larger areas. Should we anticipate more intensive and bitter community controversy? This, it seems, will depend on what can be learned from recent events and what use school officials and community leaders make of their experiences.

It is too early to evaluate the success or failure of pairing in educational terms. The purpose here is to examine the relationship between top policy-makers and local groups participating in this issue to get an early reading on community power and who determines the public policy of education. The first impression tends to confirm what Morris Janowitz already has pointed out, how little effective power has been accumulated by any one man or small group. Yet this impression must be assessed in the context of the generally elite or sets of elites who hold and exercise power at least during the intervals between elections.

This would be due partly to the presumed greater non-participation of the more distant and cynical citizens, and partly to the development of an extensive, complex administrative politics and the nature of the demand flows in the political system . . . with professional politicians in control of the administrative

process, citizens and interest groups might tend to
focus upon the sort of administrative relief that
relatively responsive, accommodation-minded professional politicians provide in their guidance of
the city's bureaucracy. [1]

The New York school bureaucracy is subject to political
forces, too, despite the insistence of the Mayor and others on the
autonomy of the school from the rest of the political system. The
slow progress of integration during this past decade reflects not
only the difficulty but the reluctance to make major changes when
to do so creates community controversy. Therefore, most integration plans have been cut down to a small-scale program that
is presented as an experiment or demonstration pilot project.
There is also a tendency to reduce the political controversy by
establishing technical administrative criteria to determine what
and how integration programs shall be adopted.

The fact that school officials adopted pairing, yet only four
sets instead of the suggested one hundred sets actually were
paired, represents the dynamics of response to growing Negro
demands, while at the same time balancing them off against local
white community sentiments. Under these circumstances educators find it necessary to negotiate in a highly volatile political
setting where power relationships between the minority and majority factors are constantly changing. Their skills in working
with both contending factors will challenge many educational principles and condition much of what will happen in the months ahead.

It becomes all the more important to identify the factors and
establish some indices by which to assess these changing power
relationships. This chapter has explored the ways of determining white parent response to the pairing through the two measures
of school attendance during the boycott and the classroom racial
counts. But the search must continue for the meaning of this evidence and for attitudes that affect integration. The behavior demonstrated on the picket lines and before the television cameras
has become a technique to catch the public eye and dramatize
real or imagined community sentiments. The two measures of
parent response, however, reflect two degrees or levels of behavior. The boycott statistics represent a short-term political

---

[1]Agger, Goldrich, and Swanson, op. cit., p. 763.

protest against public policy. The racial count data represent the more extreme behavior of resistance and withdrawal. The relationships between these two degrees of resistance must be explored further. Clearly school officials and others must learn to distinguish the various kinds and degrees of reactions to integration policies. This will help them avoid misreading parent decisional preferences and community sentiments. The first Negro boycott was hardly the "fizzle" described by School Board President James Donovan. At the same time the white exodus from the public schools needs to be analyzed more closely, as well as the ideological factors of withdrawal.

Additional research should provide the basis for some useful subcommunity comparisons in an attempt to discover influence patterns and the linkage between citywide policy-making and local response. An attempt to identify significant subcommunity factors is the task of the next chapter.

Chapter 8

FACTORING SUBCOMMUNITY VARIABLES

INTRODUCTION

The size and complexity of New York City make it a difficult place to study. Yet they offer one distinct opportunity not usually available in community studies, the existence of a great many subcommunities for comparative analysis. Rather than having to generalize from a single case, one has an opportunity to study how the same issue--in this case the same integration plan--gets worked out in a variety of subcommunities. Thus it may be possible to generate hypotheses about the relationships between the social structure of local areas, however defined, and the outcome of sociopolitical controversies.

The central research problem here is a field study of two local school districts that were proposed to undergo Princeton Plan pairings in September, 1964. In view of the available funds, personnel, and prior knowledge of the paired areas, it was decided that an intensive, qualitative study of the course of school integration controversies in two subcommunities that differed so substantially in demographic characteristics, social structure, and residential arrangements (type and quality of housing, population density) might best facilitate the development of a methodology, hypotheses, and a general model that could then be used in a larger scale study covering many more areas. The areas were Jackson Heights-Corona (Queens County) and Lincoln Square (Manhattan).

The areas represent the range of opposition to the pairing, with the white community in Jackson Heights showing the most public display of resistance, and Lincoln Square residents seeming

---

[1]This is a revised version of David Rogers and Bert E. Swanson, "White Citizen Response to the Same Integration Plan: Comparisons of Local School Districts in Northern City," Sociological Inquiry, Vol. 35, No. 1, Winter, 1965, pp. 107-122.

more receptive. The residents of the Lincoln Square area were able to block full pairing and negotiate a partial one-grade pairing instead. The local leaders, including the local school board, negotiated successfully for increased educational services. Jackson Heights, on the other hand, was the center of the now famous Parents and Taxpayers (PAT) opposition movement. Since October, 1963, this new community organization had opposed the Board's integration plans by means of court action, presentations to the City Council, demonstrations at the Mayor's office, a boycott of the public schools on opening week, and most recently, the establishment of their own private schools.

Qualitative comparisons may be buttressed by school attendance records for the two days of the opposition boycott, September 14 and 15, 1964. The average absence rate for the two days was 49 per cent in Jackson Heights-Corona and 26 per cent in Lincoln Square. These data reinforce the impression of the differences in receptivity to pairings in the two areas. More generally, however, absence data is not a completely reliable single indicator of the extent of anti-integrationist sentiment in various school districts.

TWO SCHOOL PAIRINGS:
JACKSON HEIGHTS—CORONA AND LINCOLN SQUARE

Any interpretation of the seeming differences in the extent of opposition to school pairings should be preceded by a brief clinical description of Jackson Heights-Corona and Lincoln Square. This will make an analytical and comparative discussion more meaningful.

The Jackson Heights (white) and Corona (Negro) areas are separated by Junction Boulevard, a wide thoroughfare lined with food stores, men's specialty shops, bars, and beauty parlors. It has been dubbed the Mason-Dixon line of Queens. Before the recent pairing, Junction Boulevard was the boundary line separating PS 92 in Corona and PS 149 in Jackson Heights.

The two areas differ architecturally as well as racially. Jewish, Irish, and Italian youngsters, walking along 34th Avenue to school, proceed abruptly from a village of middle income cooperatives in Jackson Heights, clustered in neat, uniform, self-contained colonies to a neighborhood of private homes in Corona, a few of them ramshackle, most of them freshly painted.

Despite such diversities the two areas have fewer differences in socio-economic status of residents and certainly more similarities than the white community in Lincoln Towers and the low income Negro area with which its schools are paired. Corona is a ghetto only geographically. There is nothing in its appearance or crime rate to suggest the slums of Harlem, Bedford-Stuyvesant, or their equivalents in Negro sections of other large northern cities. Corona's residents, upwardly mobile, are flowing to outlying regions of Long Island. Census data on Corona and Jackson Heights suggest very small differences in socio-economic status, if any, among residents. Yet many Jackson Heights parents expressed considerable fear and resentment at the prospect of sending their children to the Corona school (PS 92), even though the Board of Education spent nearly $500,000 in physical renovation as well as in additional staff and services. The white community's image of the high rates of crime, prostitution, and drug addiction in the Corona area does not correspond with data presently available and reflects the underlying sense of panic among whites. [1]

Lincoln Square contrasts sharply with this image. Located on Manhattan's West Side, it is a major site of liberal, cosmopolitan activity, with the recently formed Reform Democratic clubs and the new Lincoln Center for the Performing Arts. Lincoln House, a large cooperative, Lincoln Towers, a new upper middle income apartment complex, and the surrounding area with its old brownstones and almost palatial high-rise apartment dwellings comprise the white community. A low income housing project, some three to six blocks away, is the center of the Negro and Puerto Rican community. The two neighborhoods have little visible separation. Unlike Jackson Heights-Corona, there are large socio-economic status differences between the white and Negro areas.

Jackson Heights-Corona and Lincoln Square differ strikingly in a number of community characteristics as well as in the extent of local opposition to the school pairings. Hypotheses can be developed from these two strategic cases. However, they can

---

[1]Based on an unpublished paper by Professor Kurt Lang, State University of New York at Stony Brook, delivered at the American Sociological Society meetings, Montreal, September, 1964.

only be generated, not tested, at this time. There is no claim either to offer precise measures of all variables or to account for most of the variance in community response, but a set of procedures and criteria to measure the community variables has been developed. The interest here is in a variable-finding effort. Furthermore, even preliminary attempts at interpreting the differences in extent of anti-pairing sentiment and resistance in these two areas have helped to suggest some hypotheses, provide a basis for typing local areas, and develop some criteria for sampling subcommunities in the more extensive study.

The community data used here came from a variety of sources--intensive qualitative interviews with local leaders, attendance at meetings of the local Boards of Education, Parents' Associations and interest groups, minutes of previous meetings of these bodies, field observations of the boycott demonstrations, one completed study on citizen attitudes in Jackson Heights, and census materials on the areas.

SOCIO-ECONOMIC STATUS, MOBILITY EXPERIENCE, VALUES, AND LIFE STYLES

One may explain many of the differences in community response to the pairings in terms of differences in social background, present life situation, and social outlooks in the two areas. The Jackson Heights population, especially the families involved in the opposition movement, are predominantly lower middle class. In occupation, education, and income they belong at the margins of lower and middle class existence. A large majority are lower class white-collar workers, salesmen, or small businessmen, with little to differentiate them from many blue-collar workers except their occupational status and residential area. They are an upwardly mobile group, having moved out to Queens from ethnic ghettos closer to the central city. Many intend to remain in Queens and have very strong primary group ties in the local area. Since most cannot afford to send their children to private schools, which are regarded suspiciously by this community in any event, they would have had little means of escape from what they defined at least temporarily as a most undesirable development, namely, the pairing of their public school with one in Corona.

However, this is not a completely homogeneous white community. While the lower middle class are all of one type, there

120

is an upper middle class group of more highly educated professionals and executives whose ties in the community are more tenuous and who are likely to move out to more fashionable suburbs within the next few years. Interestingly, this group expressed both more genuine concern about maintaining the quality of local public schools and more support for the pairings than did the lower middle class element. It may be too simple an explanation to say that they could afford to support the pairing since they did not anticipate remaining in Jackson Heights. The findings of a recent study on attitudes and values of Jackson Heights residents suggest fundamental differences in social outlook between these two white groups, explainable largely in terms of differences in socio-economic status and past mobility experience. The existence of this division within the white community is consistent with the generalized set of hypotheses and theory being developed here.

But what aspect of belonging to the lower or upper middle class in these areas bears on the degree of opposition to school pairing? Actually, in the Jackson Heights area and perhaps many others outside the central city as well, the lower middle class has a particular kind of mobility and past residential experience that affected their response to the pairing plan. They migrated to Jackson Heights from ethnic ghettos that had experienced considerable neighborhood decay and invasions from lower class nonwhites. They hoped that by moving up to a semi-suburban area they could escape the hardships of central city slum conditions and enjoy such middle class amenities as home ownership, uncrowded and good schools, and safer living conditions.

Furthermore, many are members of ethnic minorities—Irish and Italian Catholics (19 per cent of the local white population) and East European Jews (another 12 per cent). They are acutely conscious of how they, as ethnic minorities, worked out of poverty and slums, coming up the hard way, without any artificial props or government support. Since they improved themselves through self-help, it seems reasonable to them to expect the same of the Negro. They feel that Negroes should do more to help themselves instead of expecting the government or some local body like a Board of Education to boost them up the social ladder.

A related characteristic of this lower middle class opposition group is the fact that they are second-generation Americans. This may have affected their outlook on school integration in at least two ways. First, many are highly ethnocentric, having moved so recently from ethnically homogeneous areas. They harbor lingering suspicions of a threatening outside world. This may be especially characteristic of the East European Jews in Jackson Heights, who still have limited contacts with the gentile community[1] and much greater distrust of such a community than it has of them. Just one step removed from the Jewish ghetto, they maintain a residue of the suspicion of outsiders that their parents felt. It is not so much that they are anxious about Negroes in their schools as that they are generally distrustful of a gentile community. These people, of course, do not conform at all to the traditional stereotype of the cosmopolitan, liberal, urban Jew and are a source of great concern to the leaders of the social reform-oriented Jewish organizations.

Another characteristic outlook of the second generation, in seeming contradiction to the first, is a degree of self-consciousness about their minority status and strong interest in being assimilated as bona fide, first class citizens. They feel compelled to assert their Americanism and to achieve recognized status as reputable and respected members of the community. Frequently there may exist an ambivalence between these two outlooks. At times there is a need for insulation and group protection from the outside world, at other times an equally strong need for acceptance.

In sum, a whole cluster of social background characteristics may help to predict what kind of response will come from a white community facing school integration. If there is a sizable population affected who are lower middle class, second generation, minority ethnics, recently migrated from the slum areas, and homeowners as well (characteristics of large segments of the Jackson Heights opposition) the community may tip in the direction of providing substantial and perhaps well-organized opposition. Such background characteristics and experiences frequently are associated with a number of social outlooks--an

---

[1]Lang, op. cit.

intolerance of outgroups, a tendency to extreme stereotyping, a rigid moralism which sees the world in terms of good and bad people, an exaggerated preoccupation with status, and a limited cultural sophistication, awareness and tolerance of alternative values--not conducive to an acceptance of school pairings and improvement of racial balance.

More generally, the kind of opposition that flourished in Jackson Heights and was conspicuously absent in Lincoln Towers may be interpreted as a form of what has been called status politics.[1] This population group is generally concerned about its ambiguous status and is especially anxious about the prospect of becoming a declasse group. If Negroes move into their schools and neighborhoods, as some fear, there will no longer be a group to whom they can point as of unequivocally lower status. The fear has both an economic and a prestige component. On economic grounds, they are concerned as homeowners about Negroes moving into their neighborhood, lowering property values, and contributing to a general deterioration of living conditions. Ultimately, many may be vitally concerned about their jobs and competition from Negroes in a rapidly automating economy. With regard to prestige, they want to preserve hard-won status advantages. Finally, on the most general level they may be expressing, as Kurt Lang suggests, a kind of zero sum concept of rights, rewards, and opportunities. Giving more to Negroes somehow means giving less to whites.

This lower middle class white community in Jackson Heights may be contrasted with the activist white group in Lincoln Towers. The latter is largely a cosmopolitan, managerial, and professional group, college educated, and while not entirely free from status concerns and anxieties, they are much more so than the Jackson Heights group. Of course, they can afford to be somewhat more tolerant about school pairings, since some can easily send their children to private schools, as studies show in fact that they do. Although many cannot afford this expense in the long run, their opposition, while there certainly is one, has been much less pronounced. The Parents and Taxpayers

---

[1]See Daniel Bell (ed.), The Radical Right (Garden City, N.Y.: Doubleday, 1963), esp. pp. 69-77 and 260-264.

groups has been unable to establish any grassroots base in Lincoln Square, as even the most outspoken opposition has refused to accept the strategies and apparent goals of that group.

Ethnic differences between population groups in the two areas, together with class differences, explain differences in both values and degree of opposition to pairing. First, there are more foreignborn in Jackson Heights (40 per cent) than in Lincoln Towers (30 per cent). Second, there are three times as many Irish and Italians in Jackson Heights (19 per cent, as compared to 6 per cent). These two ethnic groups have appeared in disproportionate numbers in opposition movements throughout the city.

But this set of social profile variables alone, however suggestive of differences in social outlook within modal populations in the two areas, is not sufficient to predict how the groups might respond to school integration plans and what the course of integration controversies might be.

LOCAL SOCIAL STRUCTURES, PATTERNS OF SOCIAL AND POLITICAL PARTICIPATION

A second cluster of variables that will help distinguish the two areas and interpret their different responses to school pairings pertains to differences in neighborhood social structure. Again, the two areas are virtually polar types and the differences are closely related to differences in social characteristics. The main difference is in the degree and type of political and social participation in the two areas in political clubs, social reform organizations, and the like.

In many important respects Jackson Heights is a microcosm of the mass society discussed in contemporary sociological writing. [1] There is an almost complete absence of intermediate community organizations between the citizenry and the city government. At the risk of oversimplification, the sociopolitical structure of Jackson Heights consists of citywide and some local public officials who make major decisions for the area and a large, powerless, usually apathetic, though recently

---

[1]William Kornhauser, The Politics of Mass Society (Glencoe, Ill.: Free Press, 1959), Chapters I-IV.

very alienated, mass. Thus, on education issues, although the opposition group now states its great concern about maintaining the quality of local public schools, in the past there was only minimal involvement in Parents' Associations and related school functions. To take another example, the Jewish social reform and civic organizations have been trying for years to recruit members, establish local chapters, and secure financial support from the very large Jewish community in Jackson Heights, but to little avail. Very active political clubs, so common throughout many middle and upper income areas of Manhattan, the Bronx, and Brooklyn, have not flourished to an equal extent in Jackson Heights. The difference in organization density between Jackson Heights and some parts of Manhattan, especially Lincoln Towers, is very striking. To cite a final example, the amount of political turnout in Jackson Heights is much lower than in Lincoln Square.

Thus there are few independent groups that function as mediating mechanisms between the residents and the system. There are no means of continually representing citizen interests and grievances to higher level officials in the city, and in the absence of such community associations citizens have no means of expressing their resentments.[1] The consequences of this for understanding the extent of opposition to school pairings and the course of integration controversies will be discussed below.

The leisure activities and styles of this lower middle class group are quite different. They live in more isolated worlds, experimenting with their new leisure in a family-oriented way-- avoiding community organizations, orienting themselves toward evenings, weekends, and vacations which they spend with their families looking at television, visiting friends and kin, cultivating their gardens, pursuing personal hobbies and do-it-yourself activities, or participating in athletics--golf, bowling, softball.[2]

---

[1]See Clark Kerr and Abraham Siegel, et al., "The Interindustry Propensity to Strike," in Arthur Kornhauser, (ed.), Industrial Conflict (New York: McGraw-Hill, 1954), pp. 191-203, for a discussion of the relation between extremist politics and the absence of intermediate social structures.

[2]See Scott Greer, "Individual Participation in Mass Society," in Roland Young (ed.), Approaches to the Study of Politics (Evanston, Ill.: Northwestern University Press, 1958), pp. 329-343.

It is realistic to suggest, then, that at least in the lower middle class areas of Jackson Heights there is a sociopolitical structure reminiscent of the Mannheim, Ortega y Gasset image of the alienated, powerless, and privatized citizen, adrift in a mass society where most power is becoming highly centralized in a few hands.[1] At the same time these people are in an anomic situation in the sense that there is no longer any close relationship between expected and actual rewards in the community, at least as they see it. Many feel that they have earned the rewards that the system offers. They have worked long hours and saved enough money to move into respectable neighborhoods, own their own homes, and establish residence near a good school. Now it seemed that these rewards were being taken away or becoming diminished as a result of social forces which they could neither understand nor control. The number of placards during the boycott calling attention to "socialist schemes in city hall," Mayor Wagner's "irresponsibility" in letting Negro groups push through school pairings, and calling for an end to Dr. Gross' "grand timetables to integrate the schools" attest to the bitterness of the Jackson Heights group, unlike their counterparts in Lincoln Square.

A second aspect of their anomic condition is the fact that they see little correspondence between their image of how local governments are supposed to operate as portrayed in high school civics texts and how Jackson Heights actually is run. Their expectations of grassroots democracy were shattered by the events of the past year, for school integration decisions seemed dictated from the Board of Education.

Thus, the absence of independent, intermediate groups to act as buffers for these powerless citizens appears to be an important condition for their strong and organized opposition to school pairings. If they had decided to express their interests and grievances against the Mayor, the Superintendent, and the Board of Education through such organizations, they would have had a built-in safety valve for venting their resentment and sense of alienation. They would have tempered their outlook as they

---

[1]Karl Mannheim, Man and Society in an Age of Reconstruction (London: Kegan Paul, 1940), and José Ortega y Gasset, The Revolt of the Masses (New York: W. W. Norton, 1932).

encountered other groups and opinions and developed a stake in improving the public schools, instead of expressing the negativistic views of the activities of the citywide and local boards of education in the integration field. For example, PAT leaders claimed in public statements a number of Board practices that never occurred--increased busing of white children into predominantly Negro areas, closing down of school for the intellectually gifted, among others.

As they realized that the pairing would take place, many Jackson Heights residents changed almost overnight from an apathetic, amorphous mass into a highly politicized, activist movement. Before the summer of 1964 the Parents' Association had been run by a minority of higher status residents who incidentally had been responsible for the pairing plan. During that summer the association was taken over by the opposition group. This close relation of apathy and activism characterizes the behavior of the lower middle class in Jackson Heights. It reflects a condition of mass society well described by Coleman and Kornhauser. As Coleman notes:

> These movements operate by mobilizing a previously apathetic mass and demanding responsiveness from an administration at those points in the decision-making process which have heretofore been shut off from public pressure. [1]

Kornhauser notes the affinity of apathy and activism:

> In the absence of proximate sources of gratification and restraint, individuals may become highly responsive to the appeal of mass movements. . . . On the other hand people may respond to their lack of proximate relations with apathy; as a result, their availability for mobilization may be hidden. Apathy born of alienation from community may persist under more or less stable conditions. However, the underlying disaffection of which apathy may be an expression readily leads to activism in times of crisis, as when people who have previously rejected politics turn out in large numbers to support demagogic attacks on the existing political system. [2]

---

[1]Coleman, op. cit., pp. 15-16.
[2]Kornhauser, op. cit., p. 61.

Many Jackson Heights mothers suddenly found themselves working together on boycotts, demonstrations, and vigils at City Hall and the Mayor's mansion. They became active in community affairs for the first time since moving to Jackson Heights.

Lincoln Square, by contrast, is a well organized community, as are many West Side areas so populated with upper middle class professionals of Reform Democrat persuasion. A variety of political organizations exist in the area, e.g., Reform Democrat clubs, a West Side Civil Rights Committee, special committees on school integration formed by the local Planning Board, and the like. Long before the Board of Education announced its pairing plan, these groups had actively sought to improve the opportunities of minority groups. This was not an alienated, powerless population, suspicious of politicans and socialist schemes generated by City Hall and the Board of Education. Their leisure activity was much less privatized than that of their counterparts in Jackson Heights, and they were much more oriented to social reform activity.

LOCAL RESIDENTIAL PATTERNS, ECOLOGICAL ARRANGEMENTS

While the social backgrounds and community organization variables may go far in predicting which way any given area may tip, still another important factor is the local residential patterns. More specifically, the extent of population density, stability, and homogeneity plus the degree to which opportunities are available for extended social contact may play a major role in determining whether or not a corporate group consciousness develops to the point of facilitating a strong grassroots organization, either for or against a pairing. The many studies of extent of class consciousness and militancy among blue-collar workers suggest the importance of these variables.[1] Only when people in very similar circumstances are thrown together to a point where they have many opportunities for sustained interaction do conditions develop for militant group action.

---

[1] See Seymour M. Lipset, et al., "The Psychology of Voting: An Analysis of Political Behavior," in Gardner Lindzey (ed.), Handbook of Social Psychology (Boston, Massachusetts: Addison Wesley, 1954), Vol. II, pp. 1140-1143; and S. M. Lipset, op. cit., Chapter 7.

The Jackson Heights case is especially instructive as to the effects of these variables. It is first of all a homogeneous community, although much more so along class than ethnic lines. Even on the latter, however, there are just a few closely knit groups. In addition, it is a fairly stable population. Many in the opposition movement have lived in the same area or co-op for several years. Some moved en masse as a single ethnic group from a previous place of residence.

Furthermore, living conditions within the cooperatives are highly conducive to the formation of a militant and well-organized opposition group. People of similar backgrounds live in a densely populated and concentrated fashion, and the ecology of the co-op where much of the opposition activity took place--in the form of meetings, demonstrations, and the establishment of a private school--encourages the formation and continuation of close friendship ties.[1] Various sites--the park bench, the low rise walls, the rumpus room--are centers of continued discussion about the issue. A "resonance" pattern has developed whereby people with similar outlooks and grievances whip one another up through regular conversations about their common plight.

Again, the Lincoln Square situation is different. The population is more heterogeneous, located for the most part in such high rise buildings as to provide less opportunity for interaction than in Jackson Heights. The playgrounds and parks along Riverside Drive serve this function, but they are far enough away from the areas of residence to allow for only limited and sporadic discussion.

In summary, patterns of friendship ties and channels for political action differ in the two areas. In Jackson Heights many friendship groups already were in existence before the integration plan was announced. Political organization developed quickly and recruited a following from within such groups. In addition, some homeowners and taxpayers' organizations also provided a nucleus for the anti-integration movement. In Lincoln Square there were fewer existing ties among local residents, especially among the

---

[1]A summary on the effects of ecological factors on the formation of groups is found in George Homans and Henry Riecken, "Psychological Aspects of Social Structure," in Lindzey, op. cit., pp. 801-805.

potential opposition, and the political organizations generally were liberal. Thus, there were contrasting vehicles for organization in the two areas--for opposition to the plan in Jackson Heights and support in Lincoln Square.

LOCAL LEADERSHIP

A final factor in the integration controversy--it might be considered an intervening rather than an independent variable-in terms of which the areas could be distinguished was the behavior of local leaders--clergy, politicians, school officials. The leadership vacuum in Jackson Heights helped facilitate the growth and organization of the opposition group. Citywide civil rights and white liberal leaders had been notoriously unsuccessful in persuading responsible local leaders to speak out in favor of the school pairing. A few local rabbis had allowed their synagogues to be used for opposition meetings. On one occasion, very much of a critical incident in the Jackson Heights area, three clergymen--a rabbi, a minister, and a priest--all offered to speak to a large assemblage of white parents at the end of the school (June, 1964) on the importance of accepting the pairing. Later they backed down, stating that they did not want to fan the flames of community discontent with more public meetings. One politician, a Democratic city councilman, took a firm public stand in favor of the pairing and now is challenged for reelection by an opponent who is very much against pairing.

Community leaders in Lincoln Square, on the other hand, frequently have spoken up in favor of the pairing. While there is not complete unanimity, a vast majority have stated for the record that they think the pairing is good for the area.

The upshot of all these community differences was that the course of the pairing controversies turned out much differently in the two areas. Jackson Heights experienced both strong opposition and extreme polarization of sides. The minority of integration-minded white parents have been all but ostracized by the community. As noted above, they have been ousted from office in the local Parents' Association. Related to this polarization is the complete absence of any moderate group in Jackson Heights that might serve to bring the contending factions together and help mobilize a more widely based coalition in favor of the pairing. The opposition has yet to change its position in any way.

A group of "hard core" mothers continue to keep their children in the newly formed private schools.

In Lincoln Square, although there is an organized opposition, the West Side Parents' League, a polarization of sides took place only briefly at an early planning stage in the controversy. At that time (early spring, 1964) even the local board of education voted against the plan. But then the controversy took a completely different course than it had in Jackson Heights. A large moderate group quickly developed, the Lincoln Square Committee for Better Schools, and it played a major role along with civil rights and white liberal groups in mobilizing a strong coalition in favor of the pairing. A later vote of the local board in June, 1964, was overwhelmingly in favor also, reversing its earlier ruling.

CONCLUSIONS

This preliminary interpretation of the differences in reaction to school pairings in the two areas contains a number of interrelated hypotheses that can be used for further studies in other areas. There is no claim to having exhausted all the key variables. One gap pertains to the strategy and behavior of education officials and local school boards in the two areas. Several school board members and some teachers have already been interviewed, but evidence is not yet sufficient for any interpretive statement as to the role of these groups. Nevertheless, the material seems significant and suggests a sharper focus for future subcommunity studies.

More specifically, two kinds of research strategy are suggested. First, an attempt should be made to secure as many indicators as possible for the variables that have been discussed. Preliminary work with census and health district data suggests that this is very feasible. Some variables mentioned--values, social and political participation--may be measured only through sensitive surveys of parents. Research thus far points to the direct relevance of such survey data for any study on the determinants of community response to school integration plans. Qualitative data on the outlooks, strategies, and behavior of local leaders can take one only so far. Ultimately there must be more than impressions of the outlooks and behavior of interested residents in these areas. Second, consideration should be given to the selection of areas for study on the basis of their theoretical importance, rather than because they happen to be conveniently located or are the site of one of the Board's many integration plans.

Educational administrators are now groping for knowledge about local areas on which to base their future policies, especially in the integration field. One finding that already has resulted from citywide interviews is that Board procedures in assessing community readiness are very vague. This research suggests that there are types of communities in which they might try their integration plans and types of community relations programs which they might follow to mobilize local support. Such help may be sorely needed in New York City and perhaps even more so in other northern cities that are not as far along in their integration efforts.

Chapter 9

PREPARATION FOR FURTHER STUDY

This one-year preparatory study of integration controversy has provided a better understanding of the educational arena. The major objectives of providing a political map and a research strategy for a large-scale study have been realized. Certainly, the conduct of further study has benefited from this year of exploration. Monitoring the events of the past year and studying their relation to events of the past decade have provided a necessary historical perspective of repetitive patterns of behavior. Numerous qualitative interviews furnished the data to assemble a political map of the participants, showing their locations in a system of constellations of satellite groups which revolve around a core in an effort to influence integration policy. Attendance at many meetings throughout the community has revealed the pattern of responses between and among citywide and local subcommunity groups, plans, and action.

SUMMARY IMPRESSIONS

A summary of impressions will present the general findings. In each case evaluative comments are made to state the unfinished business and to focus the conceptual needs of further research. In a sense these are the lessons learned during this exploratory year and they will serve to point out some of the problems that lie ahead. Four concepts are discussed below: (1) the system of core and satellite groups; (2) the subsystem of the local neighborhood schools; (3) the role of the superintendency; and (4) contending strategies.

THE SYSTEM OF CORE AND SATELLITE GROUPS

The Sayre and Kaufman concept of core and satellite groups served as a useful heuristic device to describe the structure and process of decision-making in the educational arena. Some modifications already have been made and further refinements, of course, will be effected as research progresses and they become

necessary. Several gaps still deserve comment. First, the
political map relies too heavily on a group theory of democracy
and fails to include the unorganized, the cynical, the apathetic,
and the alienated, all common elements of our urban centers.
Greater attention should be given to social class analysis in explaining the demands of minority groups for accelerated integration and the resistance of some whites to educational plans. In
fact, much of the controversy centered around the insistence of
the lower middle class--Negro and whites--upon decent places
to live, better jobs, and educational opportunities which will allow the social mobility that all desire. Investigation of class
cleavages and conflict will explain the demands and counterdemands exerted on the middle class school system. This will also
explain the origin of functional groups--the bases for their formation, as well as their goals, strategy, and tactics.

Social class analysis will provide additional focus and in-
sight into the ideologies of the major interests involved in the integration controversy. Of course, it will make more complex,
and necessarily so, the explanation of the multi-dimensional factors operating in this dispute. These should include: (1) the narrow special interests normally associated with such American
pressure groups as property owners, school committees, and
the like[1]; (2) the cultural values of ethnic politics,[2] like the Irish
and Italian Catholic, Negro, and Jewish communities; (3) the
ideologies of social change and public policy,[3] as, for instance,
liberal, conservative, and radical right; and (4) the broad political ideologies concerning who shall govern,[4] i.e., consensual
elites and competitive masses.

---

[1]For a useful discussion of pressure groups, see David B.
Truman, The Governmental Process (New York: Alfred A. Knopf, 1951).

[2]For a challenging discussion of ethnic politics, see
Glazer and Moynihan, op. cit.

[3]See Angus Campbell, Philip E. Converse, Warren E. Miller,
and Donald E. Stokes, The American Voter (New York: John Wiley
and Sons, 1960), pp. 188-215; Herbert McCloskey, Paul J. Hoffman,
and Rosemary O'Hara, "Issue, Conflict and Consensus Among Party
Leaders and Followers," The American Political Science Review,
Vol. LIV, No. 2 (June, 1960), pp. 406-427; and Philip E. Converse,
"The Nature of Belief Systems in Mass Publics," in David E. Apter
and Reinhard Bendix (eds.) Ideology and Discontent (New York:
The Free Press of Glencoe, 1964).

[4]See Agger, Goldrich, and Swanson, op. cit., pp. 14-32.

A final modification of the concept of core and satellite groups will identify and characterize system and subsystem relationships. Most of the Sayre and Kaufman description of New York politics emphasizes citywide politics and the scope and function of the general local government. It is essential to explore further the two aspects of power in the educational arena. The first is how this arena relates to the other centers of power in the system. This examination should go beyond the formal lines of authority, so well described by Sayre and Kaufman, to include the overlapping membership and activities of community influentials who display and exercise a general concern for the whole system. The polyarchical nature of influence and authority needs to be determined empirically. The second aspect, notably demonstrated in the case of school integration, is the reciprocal relationship between citywide decision-making units and individuals and those at the local neighborhood level. Local resistance to integration plans emphasizes the importance of these relationships as well as the need to incorporate the geographic subsystems as an integral part of the whole.

The Subsystem of the Local Neighborhood School

The neighborhood school is a most viable concept in urban education. The influential Educational Policies Commission recognized the dilemma of integration proposals when they stated, "It is easier to make a community center of the school if it is truly a neighborhood school," yet "the benefits of the neighborhood schools are not necessarily lost if children are transported outside the neighborhood."[1] New York City is trying to resolve the dilemma of preserving the neighborhood values and meeting the aspirations of the total community to provide equality of educational opportunities.

But then New York City has a traditional interest in the subcommunity. The political clubs played a classic role in reflecting local sentiments in the politics of the big city. Recently Community Planning Boards have been established in the 87

---

[1]Statement of the Educational Policies Commission, reported in the New York World-Telegram, June 9, 1965.

communities throughout the city. Administratively speaking, nearly five hundred community organizations are working in the field of housing, youth activities, and education. The new proposal to decentralize administrative decisions reinforces the renaissance of the 25 local school boards with their citizen memberships.

Despite these traditions and the enormous efforts to operate functional programs in the subcommunities, citywide integration plans formulated were resisted at this level. The importance of this local resistance cannot be overemphasized. It was one of the most important phenomena studied during the past year. A distinction was found between parent and community response. Furthermore, the following factors were found suggestive in explaining local subcommunity resistance: (1) socioeconomic status, mobility experience, personal values, and life styles; (2) local social structure and patterns of social and political participation; (3) local residential patterns and ecological arrangements; and (4) local leadership.

These findings suggest the need for a typology of subcommunities, using a combination of characteristics associated with differing susceptibility to anti-integrationist sentiment. The various communities can be arranged along a continuum of factors that will suggest what course integration plans will take and how much and what types of opposition and support will develop in various local areas.

A kind of multivariate model is developed here with a combination or cluster of variables that are associated with differences in community response to integration plans. No single variable can account for the major part of the reaction when the Board introduces an integration plan. Just knowing that the white community is lower middle class will not help an educational administrator, for some lower middle class areas undoubtedly are much more receptive than others.

This kind of research is of the utmost importance to both the social scientist and the educational administrator. The field of comparative urban studies is still plagued with single case studies and lacks any hypotheses, let alone theory, derived from intensive investigations of a number of areas using a common research design and conceptual scheme. The theory and hypotheses that exist generally are culled from diverse case studies

and are notoriously imprecise and rudimentary. The present
work has direct relevance in giving greater specificity and pre-
cision to theory in this field.

The Concept and Role of the Superintendency

The abrupt dismissal of Superintendent Calvin Gross toward the end of this study period illustrates the intricate nature
of the superintendency. Gross violated a cardinal rule of most
administrators by allowing the educational system to become subject to community controversy and conflict which resulted in the
arrest of local citizens who were resisting involuntary transfers
of students. These events disturbed the community, the top policy-makers, and the political leaders. His advocacy of the reorganization of the school system to a 4-4-4 plan provoked the
ire and public protest of the supervisory staff.

Sayre and Kaufman have best described the vulnerability
of the Superintendent:

> The Superintendent of Schools is the visible, full-
> time permanent head of the school system, comparable
> in some degree to the commissioner who heads the
> more typical line agency. He exercises his powers,
> however, in a more complex environment; his difficul-
> ties and frustrations are correspondingly greater.
> These begin with the barriers which stand between him
> and the achievement of sufficient internal control over
> his department to assure some opportunity for leader-
> ship and initiative of his own. There are at least four
> of these barriers. First, the Education Law and the
> by-laws of the Board of Education require a great mul-
> titude of exceedingly detailed proposals from the Super-
> intendent to come before it for reference to its com-
> mittees prior to formal Board action. Second, the
> Board of Superintendents guards the precedents and
> traditions of the system against any innovations pro-
> posed by the Superintendent, delaying its support until
> the momentum is lost, or withholding its approval al-
> together. Third, the state Education Law in its details
> (themselves most often the product of past staff strat-
> egies), and the State Educational Department as the
> statute's guardian, inhibit the Superintendent's aspira-
> tions for leadership. Fourth, the organized bureau-

cracies of the school system resist any of the Superintendent's inclinations toward changes which do not appeal to them. Against these barriers the Superintendent has insufficient leverage to accomplish much in terms of his own leadership. He must wait patiently for the rare opportunities which come his way to influence the internal organization of his agency, or its staffing practices, or its educational policies.

The Superintendent of Schools is enclosed by the Board of Education on the one hand and (unless the present incumbent is able to depart from heretofore standard practice) by the Board of Superintendents on the other, much as the Mayor is absorbed into the Board of Estimate. The two school Boards each operate in an environment of low visibility approaching complete privacy. The Superintendent must, in effect, exercise his leadership within two separate caucuses, and he cannot ordinarily first address his proposals, or appeal from Board decisions, to a larger public forum. Instead, he is under compelling pressure to preserve the outward appearances of agreement and unanimity. [1]

Gross, an outsider, fell particular prey to the system. His successor, Dr. Bernard Donovan, [2] has come up through the system and is expected to work in more smoothly. Donovan knows how the system operates in intimate detail. He is familiar with the values and aspirations of the other key members of the superintendency. He is accustomed to the need for accommodating to the diverse internal and external interests of the educational arena. This is the traditional role of New York City Superintendents, one in need of further research.

The past year in the field has revealed the great importance of the superintendency, including the principal and other supervisory staff of each school. It is necessary, therefore, to study in greater detail the educational bureaucracy as it is mobilized

---

[1]Sayre and Kaufman, op. cit., pp. 280-281.

[1]Donovan's appointment will begin on September 1, 1965. He has served as Acting Superintendent since Gross was placed on leave in March, 1965.

to implement the integration plan. Equally important is a study of the internal administrative means and styles of implementing the integration plans and the nature and extent of compliance on the part of school officials in response to the directives from the Superintendent of Schools.

Contending Group Strategies

Two distinctly different strategies were observed during the year of preparatory study. The first was a dialogue initiated by Superintendent Gross with pro-integration groups as a means of informing their leaders of his plans and working out some of the details with them. The integration leaders, however, treated the dialogue as a series of negotiating and bargaining sessions to win certain concessions and insure effective implementation of adopted policies. These two perspectives never were reconciled.

Gross's initial invitation was not extended to all parties to the dispute. The anti-pairing PAT members were excluded until Mayor Robert Wagner recommended that they be invited to discuss future integration plans. Wagner, in turn, did not make his recommendation until the emergence of the second strategy of organizing mass support through demonstrations, picketing, and boycotts. This pattern of behavior was initiated by the Negro leaders to force action by school officials and accelerate the integration of public schools. The strategy, first used by civil rights leaders in the early spring of 1964 and then by the PAT leaders in September, impressed school officials. In both cases this strategy had been adopted by those satellite groups who felt they lacked sufficient access to the core to gain a hearing or to influence the choice of policy alternatives.

Much more research into both historical and contemporary policies is necessary to understand the development of contending strategies. The conditions which cause the various core and satellite groups to use particular strategies and tactics should be plotted. This year's field work suggests the following: (1) Attempts by the Board and integration groups to win over the opposition by appeals to their conscience and sense of social responsibility were notoriously unsuccessful. Simple appeals to self-interest, e. g., that the quality of educational services in the paired schools was to be upgraded substantially, if for no other reason than that the Board could not afford to fail, were more

effective. (2) In their attempts to show their flexibility and willingness to sound out local sentiment, school officials continually
assured the opposition that the pairings were experimental. These
assurances only further alienated the groups from the school system, for they interpreted the statements to mear. that they and
their children were being used as guinea pigs. (3) Finally, the
strategy urged by many moderate groups of not having too much
community discussion in the form of public meetings, lest it
polarize the sides and lead to a stalemate, only forestalled the
inevitable polarization and delayed the process of permitting the
opposition to express its sentiments, deflating some of its extreme anxieties and misinformation.

A STRATEGY FOR RESEARCH

There is also a strategy of research. This year-long preparation has provided the time and experience to formulate a research strategy that corresponds to the three decision-making
stages in the flow of events. Stage I begins with one or more
plans suggested by school officials or citizen groups. This is
followed by discussions within the educational bureaucracy and
meetings of school officials with pressure groups who make their
various demands known and attempt to affect the decision. The
culmination of this stage is the actual development of an integration plan, referred to as the formulation stage. At this point
such questions as what plan and when are answered.

Stage II begins with the establishment of an actual plan and
refers to problems of implementation. At this time the issue becomes where and how. More specifically, it is where the plan
will be put into effect, in what specific areas and schools, and
how these areas will be prepared. This is the period of final
crystallization of policy. The field staff of the school system,
the superintendents, principals, and teachers in affected schools,
and local pressure groups are among the most active agents in
this stage, referred to as the implementation stage.

Stage III pertains to the extent to which the local area ac-
cepts the plan. It is concerned with what actually happens in
local areas affected by the plan, referred to as the acceptance
stage.

Obviously, these are arbitrary divisions. Integration is
not an ordered and neatly defined process, yet the divisions are

useful to conceptualize the sequence of events into meaningful units for study and analysis. They will be described more fully in the following statement of each stage.

Stage I: An Analysis of Determinants Affecting Formulation of Plans

The first stage of decision-making to eliminate de facto segregation of a city's schools involves research and discussion by the school officials and pressure groups making demands. Various staff personnel in the educational bureaucracy also are involved at this stage. The basic question asked in this portion of the study is: What actions of pressure groups (generalized versus specific demands, strong versus mild threats if demands are not met, broadly based versus more narrowly based coalitions seeking integration) and of school officials affect the <u>formulation of integration</u> plans and <u>the time table for their implementation</u> by the Superintendent and the Board of Education? The integration plans that actually become formulated are our dependent variable. More specifically, this section includes:

1. The nature of the plan--the degree to which it involves the major changes in the school system as indicated by:
   a. numbers of pupils affected,
   b. numbers of schools affected,
   c. cost, i.e., amount of increase in budget for services and facilities related to implementing the plan,
   d. amount of transportation involved.
2. The time table--the planned pace of implementation.
3. The extent of coverage throughout the city--numbers of school areas involved.

These dimensions of the plan are conceived as various indicators of the extent to which actual integration is involved. Thus the possible outcomes have been posited (actual plans formulated) along a continuum from very limited (conservative) plans at one pole (few schools, few minority children affected, minimal funds to integrating schools) to substantial (liberal) plans (many schools, many minority children affected, major allocations of funds to integrating schools) at the other pole. An outcome approximating the first characterization would be more in line with demands of opposition groups. An outcome approximating the second would be closer to civil rights groups' demands.

The independent variables are the power of key actors, reflecting their values, their organizational base, strategies and alliances, and the nature of demands made by community groups. The conceptual scheme that guides this portion of the study is as follows:

This stage of decision-making is viewed mainly in terms of two sets of actors responding to one another--pressure groups with indirect influence making demands on school officials with direct influence and the latter formulating particular integration plans. The relationship generally is one of inputs of pressures to speed up or slow down integration efforts from community groups and outputs of plans and their implementation from school officials. Each side is composed of a number of groups and organizations, each with a separate structure and constituency of its own that affects the positions it takes, the alliances it forms, and the speed and direction in which it can move in crisis situations. At the same time, the Superintendent and the Board of Education do not just passively react to demands from pressure groups. The Superintendent may decide to play a political role himself, thereby affecting the nature of inputs from the community by structuring the channels of communication and determining in part what power is mobilized. Or he may try to play off polarized groups against each other, in the process curbing their influence over him.

This set of relationships between the school system and community groups is, in turn, embedded in a wider socio-political environment--the Mayor and New York City government, the New York State Board of Regents and the State Legislature, and the federal government, all of whom affect what goes on in school-community relations on this issue. Ultimately they may affect the nature of the integration plan. For example, the Mayor can intervene directly, as he did during the fall of 1964 when he requested the Superintendent to allow the opposition group representation in meetings. The State Commissioner of Education can intervene, as he did in June, 1963, when he issued a request that all local school boards report to him the extent of racial balance in their schools and their plans to correct conditions that did not approximate the standards he had set. He also issued the Allen Report in May, 1964, calling for the educational park and related changes to effect integration on a very broad scale. Finally, funds from both the state and federal government (the latter under the recent Economic Opportunities Act) bear considerably on the feasibility of any plans. Thus, the recent request from the Board of Education for $1.5 billion in order to upgrade the quality of educational services may affect the nature of future integration plans. The Board's request for funds included very little mention of integration. Rather, the request was made under the assumption that upgrading the ghetto schools is of highest priority, not integrating them. The latter is seen as feasible only after minority group pupils have been brought up to a much higher level. Whether or not the funds are granted will affect the formulation of the next plan.

There are two parts to this section of the research. One is historical, the other contemporary. The history is helpful in providing more cases of integration plans evolving out of pressures from community groups. It enables us to see what kinds of plans the Board has evolved spontaneously and what kinds of demands, made at what frequency, and with what kinds of pressures, have led to what kinds of plans. The same kinds of issues are raised in our contemporary study as in the historical one.

Stage II: A Descripiton of How the Plan Is Implemented

Once a plan is formulated, there are problems of further specification. The educational bureaucracy is mobilized as the Superintendent consults with his field staff and the New York City Board of Education relates to local boards. Local pressure groups also become involved at this stage. Over the past years, for example, several parents' groups have whittled the Board's original, tentative proposal for 20 Princeton Plan pairings down to four. The basic question in this stage is: In what ways have the actions of the school system's field staff and local groups affected decisions on the implementation of plans, i.e., what areas are to be selected, what changes in educational facilities and staff are to be made in schools affected by the plans, and what techniques are to be used in preparing education officials and local residents?

There are two kinds of dependent variables at this stage. One pertains mainly to the actions of higher level school officials, labeled style of implementation. It is conceived in terms of such issues as how centralized or decentralized is the decision to select particular areas, how much use is made of public meetings

143

in areas to be affected, how much local leaders and organizations are utilized to mobilize local acceptance, and what strategies are used in dealing with the opposition. The second dependent variable is the extent of formal and informal compliance with directives from the Superintendent. The exercise of authority in the school system as an organization of professionals is not the same as in nonprofessional organizations. Professionals in New York City's educational bureaucracy have greater autonomy than the blue-collar factory workers, for example. Yet with the help of his staff the Superintendent does issue directives of varying degrees of specificity. Field superintendents, principals, and teachers in the areas where the plan is put into operation are expected to comply with his orders. In point of fact, they may effectively negate, sabotage, or at least weaken an integration plan that was developed after many months, perhaps years of study and discussion. Evidence of this past year revealed noncompliance on the part of supervisory personnel that seriously hampered the implementation of a middle school plan. These three categories of personnel are a well-recognized force in the power structure of the school system.

Stage III: Comparative Studies of Variations in Local Acceptance

At this stage the integration plan actually is put into operation at the local level. All the events that preceded--the dependent variables in the previous stages, i.e., the plan, the style of implementation, the extent of compliance by lower level personnel in the school system in carrying it out--become independent variables at this time. The major actors at this stage are all those in Stage II plus the local citizenry, especially parents who have children in the public schools at the time the plan is announced. The basic question in this section is: What factors bear on the extent of acceptance of the plan?

The main purpose of such field studies is to generate hypotheses about the relationship between both characteristics of local areas and the actions of local leaders, and citizen response to Princeton Plan pairings. It is very likely that there will be no more pairings in New York City over the next several years. Yet the hypotheses developed regarding what factors affect citizen response to pairings should apply to the degree of acceptance of the educational park. Recent interviews in local school areas suggest that the same community forces and arguments that were mobilized against the Princeton Plan pairings will also be marshalled against the educational park. Opponents of the pairing already are engaged in public discussion about the park in much the same tone.

CONCLUSION

While this is a study of school integration in just one city, the particular study is not simply one more isolated case. What happens in New York City as its school officials attempt to break up de facto segregation in the schools has relevance for every other northern city. In many ways New York can set the pattern for the nation. It is generally farther along in the formulation of integration plans and their implementation on a selective local basis than any other large city. The successes and failures of interest groups and school officials will be taken into consideration in other cities as they reach the same stage as New York. The writer's study on public housing and urban renewal, for example, makes it quite clear that policy elsewhere has been fashioned after that of New York.[1] Therefore, the hypotheses and generalizations developed from the New York experience will be applicable in other large cities. This is a study, then, with very broad policy relevance.

To illustrate these points more specifically, New York City formulated and implemented two integration plans--open enrollment and Princeton Plan pairings--before any other large northern city acted. The fact that open enrollment did not decrease the amount of de facto school segregation has already affected and will continue to affect the integration decisions of school officials elsewhere. More recently, the difficulties of implementing the Princeton Plan pairings established in the fall of 1964 and the fact that the formulation and implementation of the plans was accompanied by such a sizable and temporarily effective opposition will affect decisions made by school officials in other large urban settings. It may be that from New York's experience such a plan

---

[1]See Bert E. Swanson, "The Public Policy of Urban Renewal: Its Goals, Trends, and Conditions in New York City," unpublished paper presented to the American Political Science Association, September, 1963.

is not feasible for large cities. Civil rights leaders elsewhere may well follow the reasoning of those in New York who first pressed vigorously for such pairings on a massive scale, only to change their demands and priorities in recent months so that now some are actually opposed to the idea, preferring such other plans as the educational park.

For many years contemporary observers of urban life with either a policy or academic preoccupation have been discussing the need to know more about how New York handles various broad social problems. This study will be a first step toward bridging the unfortunate gap in the knowledge of an issue which most students of urban life agree is the most controversial and significant one in American cities today. Certainly no other issue, at least since World War II, has aroused such controversy in New York City.